MOTIVE AND METHOD
IN A CHRISTIAN ORDER

MOTIVE AND METHOD
IN A CHRISTIAN ORDER

BY

SIR JOSIAH STAMP
G.C.B., G.B.E., LL.D., D.Sc., F.B.A.

Author of
The Christian Ethic as an Economic Factor,
Internationalism,
Criticism and Other Addresses,
Ideals of a Student,
&c.

Published for the
FERNLEY-HARTLEY TRUST

LONDON
THE EPWORTH PRESS
(EDGAR C. BARTON)
25-35 CITY ROAD, E.C.1

First Edition 1936

Made *and* Printed *in* Great Britain
By The Camelot Press Ltd
London *and* Southampton

CONTENTS

5

PREFACE

THIS book has its origin in two recent incidents.
The first was the reception given by some of my
ministerial friends to the report of a lecture given
by me to the British Institute of Philosophy
under the title : ' Can Present Human Motives
Work a Planned Society ? ' In this I made a
plea that some time should now be spared from
dealing with plans and planners for a new society
and devoted to a consideration of the 'plannees.'
The contention that the limits of human motive,
or reaction to incentive, were the real limits of a
planned society was powerfully reinforced by
Professor Bellerby's *Contributive Society.* As
the aim of the Christian pulpit is that any
satisfactory plan must be nearer the Christian
ideal, and as motive is the peculiar field of Christian teaching, the transition from a general
planned society to a more Christian order of
society than we now possess is a natural one,
and the consideration of what incentives will
work such a society, and what prospect there is
of attaining them, becomes one of paramount
importance.

The second provocation came from a visit to
me by the rector of my parish, with an invitation

to take the chair at one of his weekly ' guild ' meetings to be devoted to the advocacy of ' Social Credit,' urged seriously upon me because of its closer accord with Christian ideals and principles. Any disinclination to be enthusiastic about it was interpreted almost as apathy in the Christian cause. This was reinforced by the terribly sincere views of a Methodist general practitioner of my acquaintance, thrown into contact with me during his attendance in the long illness of a near relative.

As a Fernley-Hartley Lecture this volume is not directed to economists, nor very definitely to the general reader, but rather to the younger generation of preachers. It is not intended to ' prove ' anything, but rather to suggest certain imperative considerations and disciplines which in my judgement should precede the formation and promulgation of views upon a more Christian order.

My thanks are due to the Revs. E. Harold Chappel and A. Garfield Curnow for making valuable suggestions on the proofs.

J. C. S.

June, 1936.

MOTIVE AND METHOD
IN A CHRISTIAN ORDER

INTRODUCTION

THE SCOPE OF ETHICS AND ECONOMICS

WRITERS upon one aspect or another of the
subjects suggested by the title are numerous, and
there are not wanting fairly complete works upon
applied Christian ethics, under modern conditions. It would seem almost presumptuous to
add to their number. But an examination of
them shows that for the most part they are
written by those who are highly expert in all
aspects of religious doctrine and ethics, but have
undergone a less severe discipline in economic
thought, and that, in dealing with a subject
which demands real familiarity with both, the
professional and the amateur, the vocation and
the avocation, are unequally matched. Rather
less often the subject is treated by those whose
qualifications are conversely weighted; by those
whose main activities of thought and teaching
have been successfully devoted to economic
science, but whose acquaintance with ethical and
Christian teaching is relatively superficial. The

ideas of scientists as to what the churchgoer
believes or the pulpit teaches are often quaintly
out of date, and more often an exasperation, and
useless as the basis of generalization ; but
equally, or to an even greater extent, the ideas
of many writers and speakers as to what the
content of economic science really embraces and
amounts to, as a body of necessary conditions,
are quite inadequate. ' If economics say so and
so, then so much the worse for economics,' is a
common platform phrase. The average professional economist is so apprehensive of being
drawn into fields of thought where sentiment and
wishful thinking, tradition and belief, may cloud
his reasoning, that he leans rather readily to that
growing school of economic thought which pro-
claims the objective character of his study, as
being concerned with human aims or desires as
such without any attempt to give them a scale
of values. If men are motivated to economic
action by certain forces, the economist declares
that he is not to be a judge of the worthiness of
the aims, and is only incidentally concerned with
their ethics. The engineer who builds a bridge
and calculates its stresses is not concerned with
the morals of the people who will pass over it,
or the good or bad aims of the statesmen who
may have a strategic purpose in it. Many economists declare in much the same way that they
have quite enough to do in analysing and describing the machinery of individual and social action

in the pursuit of personal satisfaction without confusing the study with a valuation or moral assessment of aims.

The consumption of alcohol, greyhound racing, churchgoing, good and bad motoring, may all have important social effects. In so far as these effects react on man in directing his consumption into particular channels, or on his productive capacity, they have an economic bearing, and must be included. But one economic man with £2,000 a year is much the same as another with the same income, independently of what 'he does about it.'

Professor Lionel Robbins has recently developed the scope and significance of economic science as a study of the relationship between 'ends and scarce means which have alternative uses' in such a way that no valuation of moral worthiness is associated with the ends and not very closely with the means. But he has done it in no ignoble spirit. It is entirely a question of the convenient delimitation of areas of study. Dr. Lindsay puts it very definitely when he says : 'Economic relations have necessarily a nature of their own, and the demand, which we sometimes hear, that economic relations should be transformed into ethical relations is, strictly speaking, an unmeaning demand.'[1] Of course, he goes on to develop the close connexion between them.

[1] *Christianity and Economics*, p. 51.

ETHICAL JUDGEMENTS ARE ESSENTIAL

Human aims ought always to be classified and examined in relation to their moral and eternal values and influence upon the soul of the individual, and also—what is not quite the same thing—upon the moral progress of the race. But they ought also to be considered closely from the point of view of their effects and their relative degrees of attainability, or practicability, in an economic sense. Man does not live by bread alone—but he must have bread to remain a man. Some moral aims or ethical principles may possibly be careless of the bread of the millions, reducing the social mechanism of production and exchange to such simplicity or such chaos that a standard of life such as we now expect is attainable only for a much smaller population. Or perhaps there is an aim which can be achieved only by a slow process of adaptation and not by revolution. Or perhaps there is a principle which is possible to the individual, but cannot be socialized or generalized. Now, the examination of this area of the relationship between ethics and economics is seldom made from the economic side at all, and rarely made by those who have competence in both fields. Archdeacon Cunningham and Professor Tawney, both eminent economic historians, but neither of them writers on pure economic analysis, are conspicuous workers in this area of thought; Dean

Inge and Dr. Lindsay, Master of Balliol, moral and political philosophers more than economists, have a great claim upon our attention. But on the whole the task is approached by a host of writers and speakers with an excess of sentiment and deficiency of rigorous analysis from the one side, and with too strong an element of scepticism and practical religious apathy from the other. The ' hard boiled ' analytic economist and the fervent, overflowing, quick pulpit reformer of society never really make contact. Each drives his track from his own side across the unexplored territory without the bearings or the instruments of the other, and they never really meet in a synthesis of effort and reconciliation.

PRACTICAL PROPOSALS MUST COMBINE BOTH

It is a great responsibility for a layman to take up any position in a long line of Fernley-Hartley Lecturers, so consistently composed of theologians of the highest rank and of professional exponents of Christian ethics, all impelled by a sense of divine vocation, and carrying many an inspired message to succeeding generations. He may let down their spiritual or emotional temperature and tension, or weaken their philosophical and theological standards. He may unconsciously twist the ' Fernley-Hartley ' tradition of thought, if we detect any such main

direction, into new and less profitable areas.
But the pulpit is not to-day confined to its
special province which I apprehend to be : the
turning of men's lives to allegiance to Christ ;
the expert exposition and trusteeship of Christian doctrine ; the upholding and constant
reminder of moral values and injunctions ; the
pastoral oversight and leadership of a Church in
which worship and spiritual values prevail.   In
other words, preaching the gospel of salvation
from sin ; authoritarian and experienced spiritual
guidance ; the trusteeship of decalogue and negative religious precept; and the shepherding of a
flock.

The pulpit is now encouraged to go further.
In many cases it is invading the sphere of laymen's activity and thought by expounding social
development, not so much by claiming superiority in laymen's specialism of thought and
science as by the authority derived from spiritual
aims, and especially the inner intent of Christianity.   In many cases this development is not
the spontaneous wish of the pulpit, but the
result of the claim by the community that the
pulpit should ' give a lead,' should be practical
and up-to-date, should deal with things that are
agitating men's minds, and especially should be
in the van of agitation for human betterment,
and no longer content with enunciating religious
platitudes.   But, however that may be, the
ferment and agitation of thought in all directions,

re-examining the foundations and assumptions and postulates of every code of action or institution of society, gives the pulpit the practical responsibility, if not of pronunciamentos and *ex cathedra* decisions, at any rate of bringing to the general fund of ideas the supremely important contribution of its own developed and Christian point of view.

It is, therefore, perhaps a sign of the times that a layman's help should be invoked in mapping, or providing the equipment for, some of the journey of the mind, which the pulpit of to-day and to-morrow must undertake. But the task is attempted with diffidence, and with the certainty that in some quarters reserve will be mistaken for cowardliness, and caution for spiritual apathy. Ten years ago, in the first Beckly Lecture, a foundation which is devoted to setting forth the social implications of Christianity, I dealt with the Christian ethic as an economic factor, and necessarily touched upon much of the ground of the present study. Indeed, I am assuming, in the brief treatment of certain sections of the subject here, that that work may be taken as an essential preliminary to this volume, for it still remains substantially my view upon the nature of the influences of the Christian ethic. But I devote myself in this Lecture, first, to a more detailed consideration of the nature of the Christian authority and its actual bearing and extent, which I then summarily took for granted; and, second, to a treatment of those particular problems which have since developed in this field, viz. the ideas of planned or newly motivated economics which are either to be more economically or more spiritually satisfactory according to the attitude of mind of the particular advocates, and the mechanisms which are being sketched for that end. In another volume, five years ago,[1] I discussed the contribution which the Christian teacher and economist respectively could make to the problems in which ethics and material well-being are mingled, and particularly the implications of the modern Christian conception of brotherhood. In another volume[2] I dealt with the brotherhood ideal in internationalism and its problems, while more recently, addressing myself to fellow students rather than to teachers and preachers, I studied the various approaches to the problem, the mental attitude and apparatus of thought required.[3] I mention these in order that I may forestall as far as possible the inevitable criticism that I have failed to treat certain very essential parts of the subject, or am oblivious of their importance.

Our younger ministers are destined to carry an immense responsibility in influencing public opinion, and if I can place at their disposal, not indeed ready-made views for them to adopt, but the

---

[1] *Criticism and Other Addresses* (1931).
[2] *Internationalism* (1931).
[3] *Ideals of a Student*, V.

results of thirty-five years' consideration of the technique and approach to these problems, and help them to avoid the many pitfalls, my purpose will be served. Throughout I am assuming purity of motive and loftiness of aim.

Archdeacon Cunningham, on the subject of the place of the pulpit in political matters, said: ' The man who feels that he is advocating a great moral cause is in danger of doing it fanatically and of disregarding any questions that are raised as to the wisdom and probable results of the particular measures involved. The clergy who are habitually thinking, not of the results of action, but of the motives which lead to it, are particularly apt to attribute interested motives to their political opponents, instead of contenting themselves with arguing as to the wisdom or unwisdom of the measures proposed.'

There is no greater temptation than the possibility of facile utterance which can meet with no opportunity for contradiction or qualification by the hearers, and which is aided by all the receptivity and charity of mental attitude induced in public worship. I have sometimes shuddered at the glib ease with which public judgements are uttered, and people's minds led to believe problems are easy and subject only to goodwill, when any declaration on questions of far less complexity and technicality in physics, engineering, or chemistry, would leave the speaker humble before his own ignorance. So my real aim is to make the study of the application of Christian principles not easier, but harder, for it must be hard if properly done. And I want also to embolden the timorous to venture his practical contribution to social regeneration.

My object here is to give some few considerations in both fields of motive and method without dogmatism, but more especially to suggest a preliminary analysis which every speaker should attempt before he makes a public pronouncement upon social problems, in the hope that we may slowly raise the standard of ultimate rightness of judgement.

The studies which involve the will and character of man are essentially more involved than those which deal with the behaviour of the material universe. The easy course is the dangerous one. My dilemma is : I would not make every preacher a technical economist or sociologist. But I would not warn any earnest amateur off the problems of economic society and assert that they are too involved for him. I would impress upon him that there are elements in them which depend upon him to a vital extent, and to which he can make an immense contribution, just as there are elements upon which he ought not to be pontifical without a mental discipline as severe as the human mind can endure, and that subjugation of his personal wishes which is a Christian surrender indeed.

Above all, we must realize that a better society will make *greater* demands upon human character, and cannot fairly be expected in advance of it.

CHAPTER I

CHRISTIANITY AND ECONOMICS
IN THE PAST

CHRISTIANITY has nearly always been concerned to change the world, either in its working or expressed religious beliefs and attitude to the unseen, the inward power of individual character, the framework of its political relationships, or the lines of social conduct. At one time both politics and economics were hardly more than a branch of theology,[1] and the theory of interest was to be found, not in any economic analysis, and not in society or the mechanism of social life, but only in authority, and that almost entirely the authority of Scripture. From the middle seventeenth century politics began to stand on its own feet, and a little later economic doctrine also started its emancipation as a separate area of human thought and examination.

The evil influences that have come from Machiavelli are found in unashamed vigour to-day in several political philosophies. They are common to Nazi thought and to the ideas

[1] *Vide* particularly Professor Tawney's *Religion and the Rise of Capitalism* and Dr. Lindsay's *Christianity and Economics*.

represented by Schleicher, whom Hitler superseded : ' Political morality has nothing to do
with human morality, he said, smiling with
almost contemptuous pity at my objections.'[1]
They are the worst enemy of this age, which is
ready otherwise for a great measure of international idealism.   Yet it seems to me that
Machiavelli did one great service, for his system
of thought cleared away the last clutter of
medieval sophistries which identified politics and
economics so definitely as a branch of sterile
scholastic theology, complete to the last button
of the whole duty of man.   The ground was thus
ready for a new and more rational structure of
first principles in opposition to the new State
expediencies.   This structure has never been
completed, and it has been altered in plan many
times, but at least only vestigial remains of the
ancient authoritarian ideas are embodied in it.

In a hundred and fifty years economic laws
were developed and postulated as iron necessities
in a world apart from Christian obligation and
sentiment.   The early nineteenth century was
full of economic doctrine and practice which,
grounded in its own necessity and immutability,
crossed the dictates of Christian feeling and
teaching with only a limited sense of incongruity
and still less of indignation.   The inevitability
of the laws of population as derived from Malthus, of rent from Ricardo, of the iron law of

[1] Klotz, *The Berlin Diaries*, 1934, p. 36.

wages at the subsistence level, gave little room
for the success of idealistic aspirations.   The
dynamic for change and amelioration by legislation and social reform, little by little, line upon
line, came mainly from pity inspired from Christian principles in particular individuals, although
there were important contributions to the movement by non-Christians moved by humanitarian
or class motives, and, moreover, much of the
opposition to the new ideas came from estab-
lished and recognized Christian interests. Socialism had an agnostic source, and the term 'Christian Socialist' applied to the Kingsley-Maurice
group is significant of the fact that the desire for
social and political amelioration and democratic
evolution was by no means a recognized monopoly of Christians, nor, indeed, any necessary corollary of Christian belief.   'There is much religion
often present in those who either do not know it
or who do not like to own it.'[1] What they really
object to acknowledge is that it is Christianity.

It is no part of my purpose on this occasion
to trace the past history of Church or Christian
influence in economic betterment, except to
indicate that the present attitude of many
Christian minds to social problems has by no
means been of long standing, but is largely a
latter-day development.

On the one hand we have such an irritating
and apparently inevitably continuous record

---

[1] E. W. Hirst, *Jesus and the Moralists*, p. 139.

of Christians and Churches taking what we now consider to be the wrong side both in war and social ethics, not sinfully but prayerfully, that an outsider might well be entitled to assume that their ethical standards have never been any true or compelling guide at all. On the other hand, there is a noble and impressive story of living strife and martyrdom for great causes and right issues that rests entirely on Christian inspiration and direction[1]—so much so that if one were to take out everything in moral advance that had had the Christian impetus and objective, there would be a very sorry residue. But in doing this we should have to include all that had been promoted by good men with ' decent instincts ' and no religious professions, who just started from the basis of thought current in their time, and assert that that basis was due to the now unacknowledged Christian impetus of the generations before—an assumption very probably true but quite unprovable. Must we conclude, then, that the use of the Christian standard as a guide or a form has been a hit-and-miss process, and that it necessarily must always be so ?

Certain preliminary considerations are desirable before we accept so negative, or indeed pessimistic, a conclusion.

First, it is clear from an examination of the evidence that ' saintliness ' in itself is no

---

[1] *Vide*, for example, the Fernley Lecture by Dr. Frank Ballard, *Christian Reality in Modern Light*.

guarantee of vision or wisdom in social and economic problems. It is not even a guarantee of enthusiasm or impetus for their solution. We can find the saints well distributed on both sides of disputed questions, now settled and generally agreed. Beautiful living and acute thinking do not always go together. Personal generosity and benevolence do not always involve wide and visionary social sympathies. Views on economic problems that will win through require detailed knowledge and some mental technique ; but the passionate fervour that converts the hearts of men may not possess either of these conspicuously. Nor have the saints always given the impetus ; a curious apathy in social affairs has in many cases existed alongside a fervour for souls that we may well envy to-day. Moreover, it is quite a modern development for the Church itself to be acutely sensible of social responsibility— that is, not merely for relief and palliatives for what the system produces, but also for creating public opinion to demand a better order. Lord Shaftesbury said, in 1849 : ' I can scarcely remember an instance in which a clergyman has been found to maintain the cause of labourers [i.e. in connexion with factory regu- lation and child labour] in the face of the pew- owners.'[1] And it is a still later manifestation

[1] *Vide* also my introduction to Dr. Bready's great work on Shaftes- bury and social industrial progress.

CM

for the Church corporately to take responsibility
for details and the scheme of such an order,
such as many from within or without would
demand, but such as many others feel is going
beyond its true sphere.

Again, the correlation between saintliness and
reform is diminished by the fact that a good
share of the reforming movement in society,
and most of the Utopias, have come from those
not actuated by Christian motives or informed
by its principles.   When G. K. Chesterton said,
' Christianity has committed crimes so monstrous
that the sun might sicken at them in heaven,'
Blatchford, in his *Clarion* days of opposition
to Christianity, said, ' No one can refute that
statement.   But Christians evade the dilemma.
When the evil works of their religion are cited,
they reply that these evil works were wrought
by false Christianity, that they were contrary
to the teachings of Christ, and so were not the
deeds of Christians at all.'   The position I am
assuming here is that we are not asserting such
an answer to apply to more than a part of the
historical record.[1]

[1] Lest it be thought that the line of attack on Christianity which
depends on examining the historical record of Christian action is out
of date, I quote from a journal received at the time of writing :
    ' The votes of these bishops, recorded in Hansard's *Parliamentary
Debates*, should make all right-thinking persons " think furiously,"
for they show, beyond all cavil and dispute, how far removed these
prelates are from democracy and its ideals and aspirations.   Bishops
voted against admitting Nonconformists to University degrees,
and against the removal of civil disabilities of Roman Catholics,
Jews, and Freethinkers.   They opposed bitterly the introduction
of free education, and voted against admitting women as members

'However true may be the case suggested so forcefully by Professor Seeley in his *Ecce Homo*,[1] it cannot be honestly affirmed that, on the large scale, the practical results of an avowed adhesion to the Christian faith make its assumptions valid beyond need of further warrant.'[2]

Second, just as we cannot assert that reforming zeal and wisdom will follow from the Christian profession, so, conversely, we cannot necessarily deduce from a satisfactory social mechanism the Christian influence as its origination.

It is not without significance that the most sincerely altruistic scheme that has recently been suggested for a new society, based entirely upon a change of motive, and such change of mechanism as that may bring about, and conceived by a competent economist, makes

of London Borough Councils. They even opposed a modest measure for providing seats for tired shop assistants, at a time when the assistants worked far longer hours than at present. None voted for the abolition of flogging women in public, beating women in prison, and the use of the lash in the British Army and Navy. The pages of Hansard show that scores of measures for the bettering of the conditions of the working class have been opposed by these bishops, and their own record carries its own worst condemnation. . . . The bishops as legislators have always been behind and against the best spirit of the age, blindly suspicious of aspirations and desires of democracy.

'The Nonconformist clergy are not much freer from criticism than their Anglican rivals. They have tried their utmost to make life " a vale of tears " for the average citizen. They have done their worst to limit the few pleasures of life. . . . This demoralizing state of affairs is largely due to the machinations of professional Nonconformity, which has always regarded all forms of amusement as rival trading concerns to their churches, and acted accordingly ' (*Freethinker*, April 19, 1936).

[1] Chapter xiv.   [2] Ballard, op. cit., p. 32.

practically no mention of Christianity, or of
Jesus Christ, either as a teacher, exemplar, or
redeemer. It could as well have been written
without the existence of Christianity.[1] Yet, of
course, it is permeated by it, but acknowledges
no debt to it, and no dependence upon it, possibly of set purpose. It is the finest exposition
yet given of the dependence of the economic
system upon average motive, and of all improvement upon raising that motive and ' evoking
widely the contributive spirit,' but it states
quite categorically that ' for such a purpose
education *is the one medium*.'[2] Spiritual dynamic
or change, or ' conversion,' or the pattern of
Christ—neither of these is mentioned. So far as
the succeeding generations are concerned, it is
not quite clear whether Professor Bellerby ex-
pects the acquired characteristics to be inherited
or not, but on the whole I think he depends on the
power of developing environment to create the
new outlook in each generation. Selfishness may
indeed be born in men, like bad manners, but he
must consider that in the technique of education

[1] J. R. Bellerby, *A Contributive Society*. Page 99 has a footnote
indicating that both the Stoic creed and the Christian emphasis on
self-denial cannot be completely carried through, but only approached.
Page 131 describes the teaching of the Dalton system as based on the
lives and words of great men of all times, with special emphasis on
the ethical principles of Christ. On p. 202 the author says it is not
an adverse comment on Christianity to show that, if followed rigidly
by all, it ' would cancel out ' ; for Christian conduct will give ' greater
balance.' But there is no direct dependence throughout the book.

[2] On p. 22, Professor Bellerby acknowledges ' religion with education as a force which may reduce the strength of self-interest,' but he
does not develop it in his practical plan.

and the social heritage of altruism it will not live.

It is, of course, not surprising that Bernard Shaw, in his picture of a Socialist State with equalized wealth, has no place for the Christian incentive. Lumping it in with religions as a whole, he is content to assure his nervous lady reader who ' has a religion '[1] that, if it is compatible with equality of income, it will not be treated worse by his Socialist Government than by any other sort of Government ; but, if it requires that incomes shall be unequal, it will be ' persecuted out of existence.'

Third, the judgement of the evidence *against* the saints is unfairly weighted. It is easy to ' job backwards.' Virtue, as well as wisdom, after the event, is rather complacent. These men, with their heads as much in the clouds as ours, had their feet in a mud of *their* tradition and past from which we are entirely free. If we believe that social forms evolve, and with them the ethics of those forms, there is no absolute ' right,' but only a relative right—a right possible to that stage of evolution. Jesuitical, you may say. But it is not essentially immoral to be conservative and conserving. The tenth person to come through the narrow aperture of the line of true advance is not necessarily less virtuous than the first ; certainly they cannot go abreast. We are recalling the great causes which have come out *right*, and

[1] *The Intelligent Woman's Guide to Socialism*, p. 440.

justly praising those who voted for them, looking askance at those who were so benighted, even if holy, as to vote against them. But there were plenty of progressives who voted for causes that were supposed to be forward ones, and that have not come right ; and so the moral stick-in-the-muds deserve our thanks. The truth is that this historical induction that we instinctively attempt is not a just one if we confine it to positive cases, to right causes that survive. Dogged conservative adhesion to ancient tenets of Christian principle has saved many a social moral escapade or experiment either wrong in itself, or coming before its time.

It is not difficult to show that many, if not most, of the great advances in human thought and emancipation from its successive prisons have been due to the religious individualists and the clerical class. A powerful generalization comes, very fairly stated, from Mr. H. G. Wells, who states that, while in theory the priest has been the inflexible guardian of tradition, he has also led almost every breakaway: the Franciscan Roger Bacon, Huss, Wyclif, Luther, Calvin, Knox and Mendel are illustrations. ' Through the scholastic clerical tradition nearly all the intellectual growth of humanity has come. The contribution to human initiative of the vast peasant-souled majority is small by comparison. . . .'[1] But of course Mr. Wells is referring

[1] *The Work, Wealth, and Happiness of Mankind*, p. 311.

more to explosive advance or change than the promulgation of ultimately accepted applications of the Christian ethic. Surely Calvin has done more to retard the ideals we hold to-day than any conservative pope. In any case the antidote to putrefaction or petrifaction is not dynamite.

LESSONS FROM THE RECORD

Let us return to the question and reword it. Has the application of the Christian standard to some social problem, by average Christian minds, judged by the past, anything more than a fifty per cent chance of being ' right ' for the future (in the sense of turning out as we expect or hope, or being approved by the standards of the future) ? There are two methods by which we might attempt an answer. We might make a careful inductive study of the past instances (where bishops and ministers, quoting texts, voted for slavery, for capital punishment for stealing sheep, for child labour, and all the rest of the sad story) and try to determine what were the moral and ethical differentiae in ideas that led them to be right or wrong, and so construct a dichotomy or category of principles (as then held) which have led men to bad, or unsound, conclusions, and to good, or sound, conclusions respectively. Then, taking the ' unsound ' list, we might probe further, and find some high common factor—such, for example, as a particularly obtrusive and dominating text, which we now find wants wider interpretation or a better rendering, or which is unworthy to bear so huge a superstructure of thought and process as they then gave it. (For example, ' The poor ye have always with you,' or, ' Take a little wine for thy stomach's sake.') We might find an outworn collocation of Scriptural ideas or texts which produced a principle whose results prove invalid. Such would be the combination in one logical whole of utterances of our Lord which stand *sub specie aeternitatis* and those which had apocalyptic limitations, or those we now see to be clearly conditioned by *kenosis,* or by Christ's humanity. In other words, we should find our saintly forbears who went into the wrong lobby did so, not through moral perversity or apathy, but through being no better scholars than their day allowed,[1] and those who went into the right lobby did so because of a slightly better or a slightly worse, or at any rate a different, scholarship, or by inconsequential chance mentalities. This, at any

---

[1] ' For the moral aspect of motive must be conditioned by intellectual insight. Those who thought it right to burn witches or to torture heretics for the glory of God were clearly influenced by the defective discernment of their day. This, however, did not excuse their own failure in discernment. Now a failure in discernment is in the last analysis really a failure in the region of motive. That torture and cruelty should be thought compatible with zeal for God, and the souls of the victims, could proceed only from a motive of which the emotional aspect had been developed at the expense of the intellectual.' Hirst, op. cit., p. 18.

rate, is the kind of impression one gets from the study of any justification on reasoned moral or Scriptural principles on the two sides of outworn controversies hotly but sincerely contested in their day.   It is not my intention to undertake this laborious inductive inquiry.

The second method would be to conduct an analysis of the *problems* upon which they pronounced and differed, in their social and economic characteristics, particularly dealing with the points of personal human motive involved, of governmental guidance and control, of technical apparatus, of dependence upon physical natural features ; and then, by an inductive study of these characteristics or elements in the problems, to ascertain whether any group showed a special susceptibility to error of judgement on the part of good and intelligent Christian men.   It might be found that they went particularly astray in judging questions where motive is dominant, because they habitually over-estimated the moral standard or perfectibility or altruism of the people concerned ;   or specially wrong in pronouncing on matters involving natural and physical questions, through sheer ignorance.   It might be discovered that, like the Rev. Thomas Malthus, they were right at one stage, and wrong at another, in the world's development.   But this induction would indicate the areas of thought in which Christian exponents ran the greatest risks in the attempt to give judgement, and it would be a real guide to future thought.

If Archdeacon Paley were living to-day, and had it in his heart to preach resignation to the poor and the acceptance of their station, it is hardly likely he would issue his twopenny pamphlet with the title, *Reasons for Contentment Addressed to the Labouring Part of the British Public* (1793) : ' Never allow our attention to dwell upon comparisons between our own condition and that of others, but keep it fixed upon the duties and concerns of the condition itself. . . . By this means a man of sound and active mind has, in his very constitution, a remedy against the disturbance of envy or discontent. To abolish riches would not be to abolish poverty, but, on the contrary, to leave it without protection and resource. It is for the poor, with so much at stake, to stand up for the laws rather than the rich. Fortunes can only by the nature of things come to the poor. Poverty means the necessity for constant occupation, which occupies the thoughts. Frugality itself is a pleasure . . . the very care and forecast that are necessary to keep expenses and earnings upon a level form, when not embarrassed by too great difficulties, an agreeable engagement of the thoughts. This is lost amidst abundance. If we bring religion into the account, the argument is still easier. Religion smooths all inequalities, because it unfolds a prospect which makes all earthly distinctions nothing.' The archdeacon shows how miserable both would be if he had to labour and the labourer in exchange had to pursue the archidiaconal studies.   The worker's life is better than that of the rich because it supplies employment, promotes activity, better health, keeps the mind engaged and quiet.   It is more sensible of ease and susceptible of pleasure, has greater alacrity of spirits and more constant cheerfulness and serenity of temper, is free from the heavy anxieties the rich feel, and ensures that children are sent to situations suited to their habits and expectations.   The French Revolution echoes in the final injunctions : ' To covet the stations or fortune of the rich, or so however to covet them as to wish to seize them by force . . . is not only wickedness but folly . . . it is not only to venture out to sea in a storm, but to venture for nothing.'   This was written just prior to the famous *Evidences*.   Sidney Lee records that Paley thought it his best performance.   But we are not surprised that it had no great success.   At any rate, record has it that Paley himself, though comfortable by the standards of his day, was never rich.

Pending a Real Internationalism

I suppose most ministers to-day would agree that tariff policy is a question of economic expediency for a particular nation at a particular time, to be judged by its effect on national welfare.   When, in 1904, feeling ran high on the political issue raised by Mr. Joseph Chamberlain, a group of clergymen declared that the salient details were superficial discussion, and preferred the 'fundamental judgements, ethical and social, which were profoundly involved.' Being charged with special responsibility for the national conscience, they invited signatures to a manifesto which denounced Protection because it 'inevitably tends to evolve motives and foster tendencies against which we are all accustomed to protest as immoral . . . no nation can adopt it without danger to the uprightness of its public life.' Whether France, Germany, and the United States took this claim to the higher Christian virtues of Free Trade seriously I cannot say. But when in due course a tariff policy was adopted by Britain, for reasons of expediency, the pulpit was silent, and there was no declaration of divine truth.

The record of Christianity in the past has its humiliations, but it also has its triumphs, and we can feel humble for the one and grateful for the other. But the more I ponder the forceful epigram that 'Christianity has never failed because it has never been tried,' the more I feel what we really mean is that the successes of Christianity in one age would be its failures in the next, because the ethic develops and the age changes it to a more imperative demand. The applied Christian ethic is an *increasing purpose*, and

I doubt not through the ages one increasing purpose
    runs,
And the thoughts of men are widened with the
    process of the suns.

THE DEMAND WE MAKE UPON CHRISTIANITY TO-DAY

It is almost instinctive in us nowadays to
think that Christianity must, if it is a real thing,
be something more than a scheme of personal
relationship of our own souls to God, and a code
of personal behaviour to our fellows. If a code
is 'right' for all individuals separately, it surely
must be 'right' for them in the aggregate, we
think, and so we proceed to infer that it can
be generalized as a code for the spiritual and
economic working of society—it ought to be
equally 'right' between two limited companies,
between a Government Department and a single
citizen, between a tennis club and a corporation,
between two trading nations. We may grudgingly
admit that a direct pattern of behaviour does not
emerge ready-made, and that the toil of thought
and prayer is necessary : it will emerge from
the principles, we think, in a uniform conclusion
reached by all men of good will. Professor Mac-
Murray says that if he cannot say 'precisely'
what he means by Christianity, it leaves him
'powerless' to make up his mind on any 'other'
social question.[1] From the multiplicity of answers

[1] *Creative Society.*

emerges a highest common factor which is so low as to be vague, and thus indefiniteness and not multiplicity is the final enemy.

It is a wholesome thing that we should be profoundly discontented with the lack of immediate contact between Christian principle and the definite social action that should accompany it. But it is perhaps unwarrantable rather than wholesome that we should expect a map of a perfect society. The common thought-mode to-day is truly that Christianity has only a ' vague and remote influence ' upon social behaviour, in contradistinction to the thought of other times, when direct guidance and clear pattern were derived. Unfortunately, almost the whole of this guidance and pattern is now thought to be either definitely wrong or else hopelessly inadequate. Yet it seems we must be always, in every age, making our attempt to reinterpret Christian principle in the light of our own conditions. Every serious student of the subject has now to admit the relativity of Christian principle as humanly interpreted. ' There may be good reason for the continuous change in the applied meaning of Christianity, but there can be little doubt that a process in which Christianity is continually changing its meaning in relation to social morality and social institutions must tend in the long run to leave the idea of Christianity vague and fluctuating, and make it fairly easy to attach it to any system of social ideas which is widely approved on other grounds.'[1] Christian morality tends to be identified with whatever is the ' done thing ' by decent people of a particular time, and therefore to be no guide, and still less a dynamic, to a better way.

Whether the past record of Christian judgement be as bad as some would say or not, we should all clearly like it to be better, and it would seem to be necessary to look, however informally and unscientifically, still conscientiously, at both sides of the task—the tools and the material. First, continually to examine and revise the ethical principles on which we rely, in the light of the latest thought about them. Second, continually to look at each problem we are judging and find its constituent elements, so that we can see how dominant are those in which ethical considerations are possible, such as motive, as against those in which ' ethical principles ' batter in vain—such as natural resources or biological truths.

The failure of the best Christian lives and minds to give us absolutes in the past, and the often unsatisfactory character of their relatives, ought to do two things : to make us very humble, and to make us examine our postulates and assumptions most carefully.

First, does it really follow that an action that is ' right ' between particular individuals can be

[1] MacMurray, op. cit., p. 12.

generalized for all individuals, and still more for aggregates of individuals acting as units ? May we not commit the logical fallacy of composition, in which, by the assumption that a whole is simply the sum of its parts and not something different from them, we fail to appreciate the new or altered relationships introduced ? We understand that A can love his neighbour B as himself, but in what precise sense can Birmingham love Croydon as itself, or the National Union of Railwaymen love the Railway Stockholders' Union, or Newcastle Corporation love the Consett Iron Company, or France love Texas ?

These are not idle contrasts or merely dialectical antitheses. Modern society does not consist wholly or mainly of relations between individuals and the community, for it is filled and interlaced with groups or corporate entities of all kinds which are neither, and have a distinct set of loyalties and allegiances. A company, through its board of directors, may do things ' in the interests of its shareholders ' (for it has power to select only particular interests, i.e. their financial interests) which the individuals or many of them would not do individually. They may be things which do not square with the interests of the community taken as a whole—such large generalizations are not its business. Or it may *not* do, in their behalf, things that they might well do individually, as *ultra vires*, e.g. make subscriptions to particular charities, exercising mercy instead of justice, and other ways of ' spending the shareholders' money.' I do not refer so much to such conflicts as are now so clear between a totalitarian State and its Churches, or universities, or other groups, or between rival concepts in nationalism and internationalism. Nor the problems raised by the objective fact in its corporate obligation, when the incident of one man killing another can only be properly interpreted in its grouping, whether it is as between one free individual or another ; whether one is the public executioner ; whether each is serving his nation at war. I am concerned more with the complication, insignificant in the time of Christ, of group relations where ethical judgement is made in behalf of the individual in some delegated area of his rights without engaging his whole ethical personality. The whole body of ethics needs to be recast in the mould of modern corporate relations.

Second. Are we quite sure that we keep the connotation of the term ' right,' as applied to one action or attitude against another, steady and unchanged in the transfer from the individuals to societies ? Is it not possible that, the relationships not being quite identical, the word is subject to some equivocation, unconscious but vital ?

Third. May not gradualness be inevitable, or, rather, the only possible line to Christian applications ? May not Christian truth be pragmatic

DM

and not absolute ? If it is, then it is not only foolish and impracticable, but positively harmful, to proclaim an ideal as essential for an age that cannot in any circumstances touch it. The best may then be the enemy of the good. A feeble ' better ' may be the only way to the best. All the past ideas of Christian application so erroneous to us may have been *strictly right,* as the only ones possible or attainable for their age. The growing child is not expected to perform the same physical task, involving weight or accuracy or endurance, as the adult, nor is his knowledge or judgement ' wrong ' because it is afterwards altered or made more adequate.

One can readily hear the objection that this is pure sophistry, that we must always preach the highest we know or can conceive, however much human nature falls below it. I distinguish. It must always be wrong to condemn others, or belittle them, if they do not join us in prescribing for common or universal social adoption plans which involve standards and schemes of conduct and behaviour quite beyond the age. The pulpit may be idealistic, and ought to be, but it should not stir social discontent by holding up as actually attainable to-day something beyond general conduct, and what in the nature of things can only be reached by generations of effort.

Fourth. A fresh difficulty is introduced if we consider the peoples of the world not merely as advancing steadily to greater heights of moral possibility, not merely as children growing together to manhood, but also as mixed at any time with widely varying possibilities, like a population of all different ages.   It is sometimes said that the pace of a cycling club is the pace of the slowest member.   Have we to admit any different practical conceptions of Christian ' rightness ' as we glance at different peoples, or do we adopt the minimum moral pace for all ? Or do we strike an average, or how otherwise do we generalize ?   Many of the practical fallacies of idealistic pacificism are based upon the assumption that men and races are ' equal,' and that the good example of Britain, in extreme trust, would be followed by all others, when actually the analogy of a Zoo in which we claim that all doors should be opened wide might be more appropriate.   There is something along this idea—that all men are *not* alike— lying implicitly as a justification behind the attitude of many friends in the Southern States to the negro problem which seems so ' unchristian ' to us who have no practical issues at stake.   We declare ' all men are equal, and the heart under a black exterior is as precious to God as that under a white, and *therefore*,' &c., &c.   But our friends say, in effect, that the colour of the skin is not the differential at all—there is *a different kind of mental homo*, as different as two distinct mammal species, and we not only can, but *must*, have different laws and moral codes, if we are to be reasonably practical in social life. And they do not readily envisage a future in which things may be different, and to which they should work, or for which they should suffer now.

Let us put a practical point upon it. Is segregation a Christian principle or not ? Should men of equal education, and working power, and personal dignity, have different waiting-rooms at stations, different travelling-cars, different areas for residence ? Are we to look forward to a time when ' all men shall brothers be ' in the sense that no distinction can be made between them in social laws and relationship ? I will assume that ' mixed marriages ' are regarded with a repugnance which has a sound though hidden biological basis, and is not due to a low standard of Christian tolerance or brotherhood. An interesting piece of study in multiple correlation has been done recently in Colorado Springs into the incidence of tuberculosis amongst white people in the different States of the Union. After eliminating the effect of six known differentiae, such as climate, altitude, &c., and getting the several States on a level basis of comparison for other influences, it is found, as might be expected from the fact that tuberculosis is generally more prevalent amongst the black population, that prevalence amongst the whites is closely related to the density of the black population in the same States. The significant fact, however, is that, with equal figures of such density, the prevalence of tuberculosis differs sharply according to whether segregation is the rule or not. Here is one of those basic social intuitions which mean more than the rationalizations we give them, based on sentiment or lack of common humanity. The dilemma may be resolved in the distant future, but it is real to-day.

Fifth. The doctrine of the Christian ' neighbour ' is almost invariably confined to the horizontal strata of time. My obligation is to love my neighbour as myself, and that means someone alive alongside me. But if we admit, as both heredity and environment compel, the idea of ' neighbours ' in succession of time, the problem of ' right ' becomes three-dimensional. Can I do a kind action to my neighbour to-day which makes the lot and the life of my ' neighbour ' of the next generation harder ? I suggest that Christian humanitarianism has hardly begun to see its duty and weigh its responsibility in this sense, to which eugenics directs our attention.

This leads us perhaps to a crucial point : have we any *right* to claim that religion, and especially Christianity, shall provide not only for communion with God, but also a clear answer to the problem of the best machinery to adopt in all circumstances for men's relationships to each other ? Those relationships are studied in government and politics, in economics and taxation, in international law, in national sovereignty, in educational and social policy, in public health. Is there one machine more Christian than another, and is it applicable in any age and to any people ? Is the political machinery of democracy more Christian than that of autocracy, of Fascism more than Socialism ? Is the economic machinery of mass production or foreign exchange more Christian than that of peasant proprietorship and the customs house ? Many will say we cannot prescribe in advance ; we can only judge by results. What results ? The standard of happiness, or the standard of life ? Or that queer blend of modern thinking which mixes the two ? We find that the British idea of parliamentary government has no marked degree of success outside the English-speaking peoples. What is the Christian judgement upon it ? How high, indeed, may we put our claims upon Christianity as a solvent of the world's puzzles ? Professor MacMurray makes Christianity stand or fall as a religion upon very comprehensive tests when he declares that, while the newness of the mechanism of life is ' forcing our activities and our *forms of human association* to break with the tradition of the past in the effort to adapt themselves to conditions,' we cling to religious concepts which are valid only for the ideas and conditions that are perishing. ' Unless we can discover a Christianity which is clear enough to be a beacon for the future, and sharp enough to cut a way for us through the tangled confusion of the present, we shall be blind guides and fireside warriors. If we cannot define our Christianity in such a way that it can determine for us a clear programme of action through which we can claim the future as our own, and fight for its possession, then we ought without hesitation to reject Christianity completely and find another faith to fight for.'[1] If he means that there is a tangle of moral values to be cut through, the test seems ideal, but not unreasonable. But he has just declared that ' people who have set their hearts on the values that are perishing, and who are dragged forward into the future by forces which they make no attempt to understand or to contest, must have their future determined by economics,' and the test of Christianity seems to lie in its power to determine ideal economic relations. Now, some sciences are clearly independent of human will or relationship—pure physics, and chemistry, and mathematics—and no one would test Christianity by any judgements as to its power to affect action in those fields. But the impact of work in them affects man and society in a thousand ways, and creates new problems to which the MacMurray test would apply. Other fields of scientific investigation touch mankind and the human will by interaction between man and matter, e.g. medicine and economics. Others, again, are a study of man and his mind

1 Op. cit., p. 15.

in himself—psychology, education, philosophy. There can be no valid claim that Christianity must equally resolve problems in all these fields; and, therefore, before it is condemned as a faith not worth possessing because it is not a supreme problem solver, with a clear programme, it might be as well that we should face precisely what we are entitled to expect from any religious belief.

I am old-fashioned enough to believe that the value of Christianity consists in the case of a single man raised from sin to conquest, from feebleness to moral strength, from meanness to beauty, rather than in a ' clear programme ' of action for unemployment or exchange control. I am also old-fashioned enough to believe that, however well the world evolves, there will always be new problems created by human relationships, for which Christianity at any given moment will have no ' clear programme,' but I do not think Christianity will therefore be a perpetual failure.

CHAPTER II

MOTIVE IN THE ECONOMIC LIFE

(1) Motive in the Present Order, a Planned
    Order and a Christian Order.[1]

Analysis of motive has generally been confined
to a classification of the types of incentive now
responsible for our economic life, and little
attention has been given either to the appropri-
ateness of the existing range of motive in a
planned society or to its adequacy. Those who
envisage a truly Christian order assume that
existing economic incentives can be replaced
entirely, in so far as they are hedonic, by
altruistic and public service ideals. But Communistic and equalitarian schemes also assume
many of the same changes, and the problem of
alternative motive is partly the same over
planned, Communistic, and Christian society,
and partly quite different. They all have in
common the necessity for examining the existing
situation. For this purpose we must consider
the nature of the economic machine. And if we
use the term ' planned society ' as a convenient

---

[1] Passages from the lecture referred to on p. 7 as given in
Philosophy, 1935, are included in this chapter.

distinction to the present competitive order much that is appropriate to it must apply also to a more Christian order. For if the ' competitive element ' and the ' profit motive ' must disappear to produce a more Christian order, this Christian order must be highly planned.

The social organism may be conveniently viewed as consisting of two parts on different planes, one the contractual, legal, and habitual relations between human beings and their work, akin to the parts of a machine, and the other the force that makes the machine work—the incentives, physical and mental limitations and reactions, akin to the motive power. If the design of a machine is radically altered, it does not follow that the old fuel and transmission of power will be either adequate or appropriate. We have to examine human behaviour in the economic field as it actually is, or has been, in our experience, and then conjecture how far it might be the same or modifiable in a social organization different from past models, and how far the new models may create new aptitudes and reactions not now necessary or developed. To put it more bluntly, whether a planned society can be worked by the existing bundle of elements in human behaviour, or whether it will demand other, and, if so, really possible, elements ; and whether a Christian order can be worked with such other elements.

Nassau Senior gave as the first of four general

propositions on which political economy rests :
' that every man desires to obtain additional
wealth with as little sacrifice as possible.' It took
an intelligible form in the schoolboy's definition :
' Political economy teaches you how to get the
most you can with the minimum honest effort.'
It accounts for the mental confusion of the small
daughter of the professor who lectured on
economic history : ' Does that mean that you
teach as little history as possible for as much
money as possible ? ' We can all think of
particular exceptions to the general principle,
of course, but the question is whether any
exception is a sufficiently high common factor
of human motive in the mass to lend itself to
generalization. The much-abused ' economic
man ' is obviously an abstraction, for few men
act on economic motives only, or even on
rational motives only, but it is a useful abstraction in the economic field which possesses
greater value or truth in that field than any
alternatives that may be assumed. The student
is always warned that before he reintroduces
the derivatives of the abstraction back into
complex reality, and makes any statement of
general force, he must reclothe the abstraction
with the discarded elements of behaviour, and
qualify his dicta. That is one reason why no
simple statement in economics is ever precisely
true. It is also a reason why Ruskinian diatribe
about ' life being wealth ' and so on is rather

irrelevant *in the economic study itself.* The introduction of moral and ethical implication at some stages in the argument is inappropriate and confusing; at others necessary and completing. Catch-phrases such as ' Production for use and not for profit,' however comprehensible from an ethical point of view, conceal, not very effectively, much confusion of economic thought, which only disappears on a careful analysis or definition of the words *use* and *profit*. Similar cloudy implications rest in such words as *service* and *needs*.

First of all, we have to consider the motives and reactions to stimuli as they at present exist—to analyse them in order that we may pick out which of them could be translated unchanged into some new sphere, which of them would have to be completely altered, and which would have to be developed to a degree that would make them almost different in kind.

Dealing first with the fund of capital that is required in any form of society which is to have a good standard of life and to take advantage of new scientific inventions, we find that, in general, the satisfaction of future wants at any moment is less valuable than the satisfaction of the same wants to-day. The discounting process of time represents an abstinence which it requires an economic price to secure. The payment of interest in some sense is a reward of abstinence, at any rate in the case of moderate

incomes ; and in any world in which there is
a measure of equalization of resources the
principle is of far greater importance than in
the nineteenth century, where we were able to
rely upon the massing of capital funds out of
wealthy resources—where the word ' abstinence '
had much less meaning.   In so far as future
enjoyment is discounted against the present,
' waiting ' requires a reward.   The price of
waiting is interest, and the quantity of waiting
may generally be increased in the same way
as a supply of any other economic product,
if that price rises.   Interest is also necessary,
in addition to the pure interest of waiting, in
respect of the risk of waiting and the possibility
of never enjoying at all.   The motives for saving
are not quite the same over the whole field.
Riskless waiting, which is what we generally
mean by ' thrift,' may be first of all undertaken
against being *worse off* in future, in which case,
by insurance, a *low rate* of interest, on the
principle of accumulation, demands *more saving*
and not less.   Or the saving may be undertaken
in order to be *better off*.   If this is for a specific
purpose, to a specific sum, then the lower the
interest the more saving.   But if saving is a
merely general desire, then the high rate of
interest as its price may increase saving.   A
high rate of interest certainly is important for
directing saving into highly profitable but rather
risky ventures.

A further motive is that of moral thrift— in an ordered life the feeling that it is wrong to spend up to the hilt; and, again, saving may be like a dividend reserve, equalizing good and bad times.

There are certain conditions under which saved money may be very plentiful, and so much more than the suitable openings for it that the price is inoperative as a control. The automatic savings coming up now through the various agencies for thrift may very easily represent a surplus during the period when business confidence is not great. The element of risk will always require a loading from the individual saver, and the price element is a controlling factor. Socially, there may be much collective individual loss but much pioneer gain. Industrially, it is no good money being cheap, unless it is also cheap *in the field of risks*. Much of this will survive in a different society.

(2) THE PRICE SYSTEM

The principles that are at work dominating economic society, and inherent in men's physical and psychological make-up, include that of diminishing utility, in which case an increasing supply can only be taken off at a less price, or additional increments are worth less to the user than the preceding ones. It is inherent

in us that we should seek the highest marginal
satisfaction, and that for this purpose the
principle of substitution is constantly at work.
I do not see how we can expect to override this
in any society, but I do see that it makes planning *outside the area of the stability of large
numbers* extremely precarious. Wages may not
be wholly determined by marginal productivity,
but it is so commanding an element in their
true level that this also is a factor to be reckoned
with, and I have not yet seen any scheme for
a planned society which gave the technique for
working it out. The individual to-day, in the
present economic society outside Russia, has
two great choices : first whether he shall spend
or save ; and, when he spends, whether he shall
buy home or foreign goods ; and, when he saves,
whether he shall invest or take risks. His
second great choice is in the occupation to be
followed ; the training for it, where he shall
reside, and the changes that he may care to
make. Now, in so far as these individual
choices work themselves out into a massive
stable result in the aggregate, the planner can
take the results for granted and project them
into the future, so that the individuals within
the aggregate will still retain freedom ; but
unless there is the compelling element of a change
of price, i.e. of interest, of wage, of rent and
transport, &c., to check changes in a mass
movement, I do not see how these chief items

of individual liberty can possibly be retained intact in a planned society. A denial of liberty in these respects must have some influence upon human motive ; exactly how much we cannot say. Just as it used to be said, with Ireland in mind, that some people would rather be badly governed by themselves than well governed by others, so, even where one can postulate a higher individual reward through planning, it might very well so react upon the individual that he would not give the service necessary to create the higher reward.

The first requirement of a planned society is to compute the probable demand in each direction, but, unless this is computed on some price, either actual or notional, the term ' probable demand ' is meaningless, and it would be best to speak, perhaps, of a computation of a demand schedule at different prices. The planner must then also construct a supply curve showing the quantities that will be forthcoming at a given level of costs. Once again a monetary economy seems necessary, with all that this connotes. On the whole, planning may be said to eliminate private capital, though it has not universally done so in set terms. But the elimination of private capital, and the substitution therefor of planned capital, which is to be a deduction from total production, does not absolve the planners from the necessity for a notional rate of interest, and for some quantitative test as to the *optimum* points of production to which to apply their capital.

I have not so far seen any successful attempts to avoid the usual market-price test. Let us suppose that the consumer is prepared to give up the equivalent of x hours of his labour to procure the product of x hours of somebody else's. If there is a change in his tastes and he will only give x hours minus 1 for one hour's labour, then there is over-supply, and price must come down. But if the consumers are keen, and will give x plus 1 hours, then the price ought to go up, and, in consequence, supply should increase. But a plan states how much capital is going into the production and also how much labour, and, therefore, the entry of labour into the industry is controlled, and I imagine that wages must also be controlled if they are not to be so sensitive as to keep the numbers down. So long, therefore, as people can give effect to a slackened or increased desire for any product, or so long, indeed, as nature itself varies the supply, and it can only be accommodated by changes in demand, I find it very difficult to secure a satisfactory plan. In the second place, the consumers' choice may be affected in the endeavour to make rational the necessary international trade, and thus not to upset the plan. Supposing that hats are to come from Paris which are preferable to the British. They must either be kept out and the consumers' choice affected, or,

Em

if they come in, the plan is upset. Fashion and obsolescence are put into strait-jackets. I understand that the crocodile-leather and snakeskin shoes of the lady visitors in Moscow have caused more flutters in the breasts of the Russian girls than that distinction would in our minds actually deserve.

In the third place, invention and risk under a planned scheme have to be dealt with by committees subject to political attack. They must be judged by results. The question is, how soon? And are these results to be collective or individual? Will one good success be a complete answer to three failures? Modern competitive enterprise, with all its disadvantages, constantly seeking novelty, does get us forward in one way or another. It is a question whether, in the long run, the attitude of mind which is more bent upon establishing stability and standardization will not keep back economic development. Certainly all human motives of management, as we know them now, will want to ' justify ' the plan, and this may tend to mean more to them than would breaking the plan and so giving the greater ultimate advantage. On the assumption that the consumers maintain a good freedom of directing their purchasing-power, can the managers compete by advertisements and other blandishments? The increasing real wage of the average wage-earner is at the present moment enlarging the scope for expenditure upon travel by bus or

train.   This is greatly sought and competed for,
not merely amongst the different agencies for
travel, but as against other ways of spending the
money, and probably as severe a competitor for
money spent in evening excursions as any other
would be the campaign for spreading the habit
of beer-drinking.   How, under a planned society,
will these rival attractions for increasing purchasing-power be resolved ?

(3) MOTIVES AND INCENTIVES IN PERSONAL WORK—WAGES

The motives which affect the output of the
mass of the workers must be of paramount
importance.   In this country they are wage-
earners.   Their reactions to different stimuli
are notoriously not the same in all countries or
in all ages.   In Great Britain, apart from the
differential higher return that is normally expected for greater skill and responsibility, it is
generally suggested that an increase in earnings
will also increase effort and willingness to produce, i.e. the higher price creates a larger supply ;
conversely, that a lower return reduces the
amount of effort forthcoming, but, on the other
hand, with business on competitive lines, that
more people can be employed at the lower wages.
To these generalizations there are numerous
exceptions ; in so far as they are true, they are
true only for movements at a particular time and

not for changes which are absolute over long
periods. It would be ridiculous to say that
because men are now paid four, or perhaps five,
times as much as they were a hundred years ago,
they are willing to work four or five times as
hard. Generalization also ignores the fact that
the higher and lower rewards respectively may
have physical consequences as distinct from
psychological, and that the higher yield of output from a higher wage return may come from
better health and physical capacity rather than
from psychological willingness to do more.
From a broad point of view, the best test is
perhaps that of a relation between wage and
effort as found in piece rates, but the quantitative connexion between the two is never exact.
If wages are well above the recognized subsistence level, a fixed addition is certainly not
correlated to an increase of effort. Often a standard amount per week is looked for, and if, by
a change of rates, it can be got with fewer hours,
then leisure is preferred, or slackness may set in,
and ' Monday is a bad day.' This has been
verified again and again. In the present state
of average psychology, a rise in *real* wages is of
less importance than a rise in money wages, and
a rise in real wages may be quite inoperative in
securing increased production. A *fall* in money
wages is quicker to work a change than a fall in
real wages, and also may lead to disputes and
stoppages. As I have said, the absolute rate of

real wages is not very material, whether we judge it by comparisons over periods of time, or country by country. It is the comparative rate in a man's own trade over short periods, or compared with the adjoining trades, that has psychological value in effort. Perhaps quite as important is the appearance of a disparity in large payments going to the other factors of production, and a wage that may be consistent with contentment and maximum effort at one period may mean merely discontent and slacking if there is the appearance of large profit going in other directions. Economic psychology is by no means uniform throughout the world. I remember being told, when we were discussing in 1924 on the Dawes Commission whether the German railways should be a Government concern or under private management, that the uniform denoting Government service was worth a definite differential in money. There are, no doubt, in all ranks, elements of prestige which may in themselves act in the same way as an increment or decrement of money. There is a marked increase in the extent to which pride of success and of craftsmanship are operative beyond the monetary incentive to produce good and plentiful work. There is, too, the pride of institution, particularly if it can be put competitively, and, just as the members of a family may quarrel amongst themselves, but will stand together like a rock if it is a question of contest with another family, so the different factors in a single business may pull away from each other if the issue is a domestic one, but can be made to play up for the honour of the company or the concern or the district if there is a rival institution. In the commercial and operating departments of the L.M.S Railway they have done their best to bring into operation this factor of friendly rivalry within the vast area of the railway by giving quotas to separate units or places in the different districts and setting the places and districts respectively against each other like football teams in a league table. It is a matter of fact that this appeal to the sporting or competitive instinct works marvels in stimulus. The possession by a station of the shield of the district for the year is a matter of pride much more acute than the possession of the cup by a larger area. Over a certain area of the wage-earning class there is an element of ambition which leads to a desire to excel and rise out of the ranks, but this is not assisted in the main by trade union ideas ; nor is it very operative after a few years. My own observation leads me to the view that there is enough of it to bring out a number of leaders, but not enough to increase the mass output, on a large scale, of all workers taken together.

The incentives that may be counted upon to work successfully in an untried order of economic society can only be the subject of guesswork,

ising at its best to reasonable inference. By
passing in review the actual incentives of the
results of which we have factual experience, we
may discern some existing, even germinally,
which may by encouragement and wide adoption
serve that higher purpose. At any rate, the
first responsibility of the reformer is to study the
known before he ventures to be dogmatic about
the unknown, and to endeavour to classify incentives according to differences of ethical or moral
import as well as their merely economic efficiency, in order to see whether, in a higher order
of society, those upon which he relies will reach
a right Christian standard as well as perform the
more prosaic task of ' working the machine.'
I propose to set out a brief classification of the
present economic stimuli to effort, dealing first
with all those which come under the wide head-
ing of *wages*. Whether we speak of ' wage
slavery ' or not, some examination of the different elements of reward, and their different
effects, is an essential basis of further constructive thought.

We need not spend time in covering the
history of wages, except to say that piece wages
or wages by output were found in the Middle
Ages, widely used but never predominant. Objections to incentive to output have often been
due to the technical difficulties of measuring output fairly; sometimes the materials and conditions
vary too much, sometimes there is a baffling

interdependence of workers. But, even where no difficulty of judgement or standard exists, these incentives have been disliked because they lead to over-exertion or too great a zeal for gain, as against the claims of physique and leisure. Organized labour has objected to piecework wages because the system tends to make the individual depend more on his own efforts than upon collective uniform bargains by unions. In particular cases one can never be positive about the likelihood of success ; in some concerns workers would not regard any time-payment system as ' fair.' Often objections are based on the experience of rate-cutting in the past ; the system is regarded as luring the worker on to show just how much can be produced under pressure, and then taking advantage of this knowledge to reduce rates so that that amount *must* be produced to yield a living wage. This suspicion has been allayed by establishing rules against change of rate in the absence of real changes in operation. Sometimes union leaders have endeavoured to get high earnings at piecework fixed as standard earnings on a time basis, but the movement has been defeated by the workers. Apart from doubts about methods of computation, opposition to output incentives has come from the habitually lazy. Before the introduction of carefully measured standards of production, the distinction between the good and the poor producer was not so clear-cut. When there is no

particular incentive, apart from the indefinite
hope for a higher rate or for ultimate promotion,
there is a tendency toward the maintenance of
an accepted and not very high rate of output.
When it is made worth while for the competent
and industrious worker to increase his output,
the lazy man appears at a disadvantage. Unable
or unwilling to qualify for the higher earnings, he
resents the demonstration of his inferiority, and
objects strenuously to what he terms the in-
human speed demanded by the incentive system.
Time wages are of various kinds : (1) the
' straight ' wage per hour, day, or week, regardless of specific output ; (2) a standard wage,
where an output indefinitely below a standard
commands one rate, and an output indefinitely
above it another rate ; and (3) time rates graded
in more steps for different stages of productivity.
These time wages give all gains and losses to the
wage-payer. In the second class, the wage-
earner gets all the direct differences resulting
from his effort : (1) direct piece rates at settled
prices ; (2) higher piece rates for higher outputs ;
(3) complex combinations of time rates and piece
rates.

But the third class includes many devices,
more or less complex, for sharing the direct savings between worker and employer. They have
their inventors' names, Bedeaux, Stevens, &c.,
and the choice depends upon the class of factory
and the possibility of standardizing performance.

An American investigator[1] has made a useful nine-point classification :

(1) The simple time wage, with the limits of dismissal for inefficiency at one end or promotion for excellence at the other. If careful records are kept, and rates adjusted, this may be as effective as the complex systems. It is, of course, the only type applicable to many cases, and is the most widespread.

(2) The multiple time rate, e.g. a straight time rate for output up to the standard, plus a 20 per cent bonus for time saved above the task. This is especially useful for group work.

(3) Straight piece rates—the most generous to good workers and hard on beginners, and most useful for steady work on independent repetitive operations. Its greatest difficulty is the accurate setting of rates, and good faith in the changing of them.

(4) The Merrick or Multiple Piece Rate Plan. The piece rates increase at special points as output increases. The method affords ' continuing incentives for workers who are improving ' ; it is simple and an advance on straight piecework.

(5) The Gantt Task and Bonus Plan. This puts together a time rate and a high piece rate, by giving time wages until the standard task is reached, at which point the increase is from 20 to 50 per cent. It avoids low wages for the less efficient with a strong incentive for the best workers, and is especially useful for the working of expensive machinery.

(6) The Halsey Premium Plan is usually optional. It sets a low standard of output for time wages, and gives 50 per cent of the savings made above the low level.

(7) The Bedeaux Point Premium Plan is like the

[1] Charles Lytle, of New York University.

foregoing, except that the standard task is higher, and the workers get 75 per cent of the savings. Time wages apply up to the standard. It is said to be valuable where there is diversity of operation in large-scale business.

(8) The Barth Variable Sharing Plan is more mathematical than Nos. 6 and 7, paying less than the Halsey Plan for high output.

(9) The Emerson Efficiency Bonus Plan is used for a gradual change from time to high piece rates. Time wage is guaranteed up to two-thirds of a high standard, with bonuses increasing up to 20 per cent at the standard. It is simple, and attractive to beginners, and can easily be combined with time rates.

A statistical investigation by means of a large sample showed that the percentage of workers paid by time had remained constant over eleven years, but that premium bonus systems had declined in favour of straight piece rates. Piece rates were much more prevalent in particular industries, and in medium-sized as against large and small concerns ; 56·3 per cent of the wage-earners had straight time wages, 16·4 per cent had individual piece rates, 5·7 per cent group piece rates, and 21·6 per cent had premium and bonus plans. But the percentages of the number of concerns paying the various rates were quite different : 22·8 paid straight time rates, 36·3 a combination of time and piece rates, and only 1·3 per cent paid piece rates only ; 37·5 per cent included bonus plans. It seems that the methods of arriving at standard performances and piece rates are of great importance.   About a third of the concerns used an average of past records, and 40 per cent claimed to make detailed time-study analysis.   Central time-study departments are growing in favour compared with estimates by foremen. The charge frequently made that under incentive systems the pace is set by the best worker, so that average workers have to work under undue pressure to get a reasonable wage, is denied emphatically in this investigation.   Two-thirds of the concerns definitely claimed to use the average worker only as a standard, the others admitted the ' expected accomplishment of thoroughly trained and experienced workers.'   The practice of extending incentive systems to foremen and supervisors is growing with experience—the bonuses extend to rewards for increased production, improved quality, reduced costs, less waste, and increased profits.

It is said that the 1929–33 depression tended to increase bonus plans, for the National Recovery Act introduced higher wages and shorter hours, and so the higher unit costs had to be met by improved output per man.   But this was by no means universal, for some soon dropped incentive plans as unworkable under a system that prescribed high minimum wage rates.   It was also reported that piece rates were no longer effective, because workers were well enough satisfied with the minimum wage to prevent them from exerting themselves sufficiently to earn a larger amount possible under piecework.   Under the N.R.A. the chief factors against these incentive plans were the minimum wage rates and union opposition.   Sometimes they have caused labour trouble—protests against the payment of bonuses to foremen, movements for or against group rates, and general difficulties in adjusting rates to the satisfaction of all.   But the majority of employers find that incentives have been a factor in maintaining good will, and any attempt to remove them would be greeted with protest, even to striking.   There is often initial opposition, succeeded by approval.   Workers often like to make up a loss of earnings caused by reduction of hours.   One employer said, ' The more intelligent and the more skilled a worker is, the greater is his appreciation of this wage incentive plan, in that the basis for his increased compensation is an accurate measurement of work accomplished rather than the more or less superficial judgement of his supervisors.'

Formidable opposition to the extension of incentives is seen in the growth of power of organized labour under the National Recovery Act.   Labour unions have always been antagonistic toward incentive systems, because these systems emphasize efficiency, and make it possible for a worker to determine his own earnings without assistance from the outside.   Already organized labour has indicated the continuance of this opposition by making the elimination of incentive systems a condition of peace in some recent labour disputes. Some employers report that in plants or departments recently organized, the unions are trying to stir up opposition to incentive plans that for years have worked satisfactorily and have won the complete approval of the employees involved. But those who feel that bonus systems must be continued urge that workers have been made so inefficient, and have acquired such a distaste for steady work, as a result of their connexion with relief jobs of one kind or another, that there seems to be a general feeling, fostered by Government policy, that a man is entitled to a living without working for it. Industry is already feeling the effects of this psychology in the attitude of long-unemployed workers who have been re-employed. To overcome this feeling, ambition must be rekindled by making high earnings available only to those who work for them, and the most effective means for accomplishing this is thought to be the use of wage incentives.

In addition to the schemes which have been referred to, there are always special bonus arrangements when profits are good, rewarding merit, reduced costs, increased production or sales : but these are not according to any clear rule, and cannot be classified.

The opinion of the majority of business execu-

tives in the United States may be classified thus :
The reasons for expecting a more general use of
incentives include :

(1) To provide a more equitable distribution
of income from manufacturing.

(2) To counteract indolent habits fostered by
unemployment and relief methods.

(3) To increase productivity of high-priced
machinery in order to make its use profitable.

(4) To build up a highly efficient working force
of minimum size in order to reduce the costs of
impending social insurance taxes on industry.

Executives who expect the use of wage incentives to decline believe :

(1) That the present emphasis on re-employ-
ing as many persons as possible is directly
opposed to the principle of incentives, which is
to increase productive efficiency.

(2) That incentives are most needed in times
of labour shortage, and indications point to the
probable availability, except in certain lines, of
plenty of labour for some time to come.

(3) That the proper functioning of incentives
requires a steady flow of work, and business
conditions at present make this impossible.

(4) That the enhanced strength and prestige of
organized labour unions will make the opposition
which they long have shown toward these
systems more effective, and that fear of such

opposition will deter from introducing incentive plans employers who otherwise would be likely to do so.

Two significant developments in manufacturing technique which tend to diminish the need for incentive systems are what might be termed the conveyor-belt method[1] of regulating the rate of output, and the growing practice of establishing careful performance standards in connexion with work performed on an hourly rate basis.

It cannot be fairly said that in this country trade unions have been generally unwilling to recognize the validity of differences of earnings. They have often insisted on standard *rates* of payment for identical work, which can easily result in very different total earnings. But time work is often the objective, and a standard rate, at time work, must necessarily lead more often to uniformity of earnings not closely related to actual output. Over thirty years ago the Webbs referred to the ' deeply rooted conviction that the conscientious, industrious, and slow mechanic ought in equity to receive no less pay than his quicker but equally meritorious neighbour.'[2] But this could be found to be based on the conception of uniformity in the rate, and the apparent divergences of view were to be reconciled by studying the *operations* involved

[1] In this the object of the work proceeds past each worker at a regulated speed giving him just time enough to ' do his bit ' upon it before it is out of reach.

[2] *Industrial Democracy*, p. 285.

in the two classes of case.   They gave a list of
38 unions insisting on time work, of 49 insisting
on piecework, and 24 which willingly recognized
both kinds in different departments, and they
were the first to show how the opposite attitudes
could arise from a common unexpressed feeling.
But particular unions were quite unconscious of
the principle upon which their empirical action
had been based.   'The same unconsciousness
sometimes leads to a persistence in whichever
method of remuneration has been customary,
long after the circumstances have changed.'[1]
The whole psychology is very complex in its
manifestations, and the subject in its practical
details is too vast to be covered here, and must
be studied in the appropriate specialized literature.   The Webbs quote a rule of the Bradford
Lodge of the Labourers' Union of 1867 :   'You
are strictly cautioned not to outstep good rules
by doing double the work you are required and
causing others to do the same, in order to gain a
smile from the master.'   Since that time the
subject of restrictions, written or understood,
has caused recriminations far and wide, and the
objects have been widely misunderstood—they
have by no means always been intended to produce a deadening equality for its own sake, but
have been the natural corollary of a standard
rate for standard work.   In essence they have
resembled the vendors' instinct to get together to

---

[1] *Industrial Democracy*, p. 301.

F M

protect a fair price from that wanton under-
cutting which they regard as subversive of the
stability of the whole trade, and therefore of the
ultimate public advantage. There is nothing
less ethical about those restrictions which preserve the integrity of a rate of wage than those
arrangements which agree upon a fair price.
But, of course, not all restrictions have been of
this order, and when they have restricted output
paid by piece rates, and have not a basis in safe-
guarding health, their ethical and economic
justification is much harder to find.

(4) THE RUSSIAN EXPERIMENT IN REWARDS

An ounce of practice is worth a ton of theory.
But, unfortunately, we have no comprehensive
example of the attempt to work an economic
society with an abolition or modification of
differential rewards as incentives, except that of
Russia for a short time. This example has for our
purpose several good features and several bad :

(*a*) The good features include the fact that the
new régime succeeded one of economic barren-
ness and poverty, with a low standard of life.
Almost any new and thought-out leadership had
more chances of success than of failure in bettering such a predecessor. Improvement might be
due to many different causes, but it should not
be difficult to persuade the millions that much of
it resulted from a particular feature in the new
scheme, such as the establishment of equal wages,

or other signs of economic equality.   It would
have been a much more difficult problem if the
system replaced had been one which yielded a
good standard of life, and the new political
system needed to be much more perfect to show
tangible improvements upon it.   Then every
feature of novelty would have come under criticism and challenge.   From this point of view of
a chance of success by comparison, the Russian
experiment was most favourably placed.

(*b*) The appeal for the new incentive in
' service ' to the State or humanity has been
worked with every device of psychological per-
cussion upon the minds of a simple and impres-
sionable people.   On taking away the differential
profit motive to betterment or good work, they
were not left with a psychological vacuum, but
a real objective took its place.

(*c*) But, unfortunately for our purpose, this
objective was imposed from without, and was
not the spontaneous or educated wish of the
individual soul.   No one can say that the
millions of Russia gave up economic incentives
and chose the alternative ideals of ' service ' by
personal acts of will and altruism.   Now, the
Christian order would not wish to prescribe and
dragoon ; it would evoke and generate.

(*d*) Again, the substituted idea of service for
humanity is not based on any religious foundation at all.   It is frankly independent of religion,
and even hostile to it, and it is, therefore, not a

good test case of what might be accomplished in a more Christian order by abolition of differential economic incentives.

(*e*) Perhaps the most difficult feature is that the experiment in pure non-differentiation was so short, and introduced at such a difficult time. But, for what it may be worth, what is the lesson of the Russian experiment on this subject ?

In December 1918 the Code of Labour was issued. Labour was declared to be a public duty ; the workman had a right to get his ' labour ration,' and not ' wages,' which were an attribute of the capitalistic régime. ' Equal remuneration for all workmen ' was the slogan, and there was to be no difference in the remuneration for skilled and for unskilled labour.[1] The first consequence was that ' all skilled labour broke down.' By February 1921 pure socialization was complete in detail, but the Nemesis was swift, and a completely new economic policy followed in the same year. The results of the abolition of differentiation in remuneration were disastrous, and the number of skilled labourers diminished greatly. With the National Plan great stress was laid on artificially stimulating the efficiency of labour and quantity of output. Therefore, ' wherever possible the system of piecework wages has been introduced. This was a most powerful device for increasing production, although it was, of course, contrary

[1] Paul Haensel, *The Economic Policy of Soviet Russia*, p. 29.

to Socialistic conceptions.'[1] They then went
so far in 'inducements' that quality suffered,
and new ideas were introduced. 'One cannot
help thinking that in Soviet Russia exploitation
of the workman is practised in various and most
ingenious forms.' In December 1930 a special
order, signed by the praesidium of the Central
Council of Trade Unions and the Supreme
Council of National Economy, sought to regulate wages by the utmost possible application
of piecework wages and by forcing skilled
labourers to remain in their respective factories.
They also adopted many shock devices universally condemned by all traditional trade-union
practice.[2] Differential systems of prices for
goods did much to confuse and baffle these
money incentives, but these are now being
abolished. The elaborate system for giving a
different value to the rouble for different classes
of workers has developed and a worker's ration
card indicated how much he was entitled to get
from the 'cheap shop.'

Gradually, by returning to capitalist devices
and incentives, the Soviet Government prepared the way for the Stakhanovist movement,
which has now swept western Russia. 'It
is significantly a workers' movement, originating
from the shining example of Alexei Stakhanov,
a stolid, good-humoured miner in the Donetz

[1] Haensel, p. 104, and Brutzus, *Economic Planning in Soviet Russia*,
p. 105 (1930).
[2] Haensel, 'Labour under the Soviet,' in *Foreign Affairs*, April 1931.

coal-mines, who discovered that by working hard, and giving all specialized jobs to those best suited to do them, much more coal could be hewn in a day than by the old eye-on-the-clock methods.'[1] ' The readiness of the workers to initiate, and of the Government to advance, an increase in productivity, distinguishes the Stakhanov movement from the Taylorism, Bedeauxism, or technology of other countries, which are only varying methods to increase productivity by the scientific exploitation of labour. . . . It represents thus, not only a revolution in technique, but also in human relations, conceptions, and a fundamental change in the whole basis of society.'[2]

The Stakhanov movement had a great influence on the development of the Russian plan in 1935. Stalin said at the Stakhanov Conference that emphasis must now be laid upon ' workers who have mastered technique.' The much greater advance in 1935 was due not merely to the natural fruition of earlier efforts, but to the new conception of what was lacking in Russian economy. ' Of decisive importance . . . was the repeal of the card system for bread and other products, and the substitution of a transition to new prices in place of the system of supplying goods for agricultural deliveries to the State. The abolition of the cards and the

[1] *The Times*, ' The New Phase in Russia.'
[2] *Monthly Review*, issued by U.S.S.R., April 1936, p. 198.

establishment of uniform prices for food products made the money form of wages the chief stimulus for the worker. Progressive piece rates of labour quickly began to be introduced in factories and plants. These played a great rôle in the development of the Stakhanov movement. Without . . . the strengthening of the part played by wages . . . and especially the progressive piece rates of labour, we would not have had such a rapid development of the Stakhanov movement. The interest of the workers in increasing their wages was of no unimportant significance in the development of the Stakhanov movement, and, indeed, the earnings of Stakhanovites became record earnings.'[1] Stalin refers on the same occasion to the rapidly improving standard of life due to this innovation. For 1936 the plans include a wider application of ' progressive piecework and premium systems of payment for labour.'

Dr. S. P. Turin, who has made an exhaustive study of the economic progress of Soviet Russia,[2] says that the reintroduction of piece work, giving better chances to earn more, produced a tremendous increase in productivity of labour and output. The workers tend to prefer overtime to leisure, where it is paid. They are interested in producing more in Russia than in a capitalist country, because they consider their

[1] Speech by V. M. Molotov, Chairman of the Council of People's Commissars of the U.S.S.R., on ' The Plan and our Tasks.'
[2] Vide particularly, From Peter the Great to Lenin.

work as a real partnership, giving them more chances of promotion. Yet ' sanctions ' are largely applied, and the management has to have dictatorial power in insisting on the fulfilment of collective agreements, which are such that no one can really carry them out to the letter.[1]

For some time past the differential wage given to skilled workers has been increasing, and the number of those entitled to it has also become greater with more experience. In 1924, 64 per cent of the population received 40 roubles a month, but in 1930 it was only 10 per cent. The most highly paid, with a wage of over 150 roubles a month, increased from 0·1 to 7·6 of the total.[2] ' In capitalist countries, limits are set to the workers' consumption by the price of his labour (his wages), but in our economy these limits are set by the productivity of labour.'

We are told that the present action over individual incentive is only an interlude, and, when the standard is high enough, the old ideas of equality throughout will be resumed. But the young are being encouraged in individualistic habits, and they see their elders with ' high salaries and great privileges.'[3] One doubts whether this phase will be so easily unlearnt, and whether they are likely to forgo individual profit for flat uniformity.

[1] Letter to the author.
[2] J. A. Kraval, Assistant People's Commissar for Labour, *Financial News*, Russian Supplement, June 6, 1932.
[3] Ibid.

Sidney and Beatrice Webb have their own important estimate of the Russian experiment, and it is clear from their great work that this order, so completely the antithesis of our own, is working out to some new equilibrium which we can neither ignore nor despise. He says that Soviet Communism ' does not mean, and never has meant, equality of wages, earnings, or shares. The Soviet Union to-day does not pretend to be a Communist community, nor even a completely Socialist community ; but only to be on the way thither.'[1] There is no sign of any tendency towards equality of wages, salaries, or shares. ' It is the authors and artists who make the large incomes '—the high officials get salaries about equal to wages earned at piecework by a skilled craftsman. The Webbs have given an impressive picture of a new order in the making, but the last claim they would make for it is that it is a Christian order.

The Salaried and Professional Classes

Passing from Russian to general conditions the lower ranges of salary are governed by conditions similar to those affecting wages, and are not easily distinguishable. But the larger salaries of business administration are not explained or controlled by the same principles. There is no force at work which makes it possible

[1] Lord Passfield in *International Affairs*, 1936.

for a managing director to secure the 'marginal productivity '[1] of his efforts ; if he is productive at all, he will certainly almost always get far less.   One may say that there is a certain minimum for each responsible post, which represents that addition to a salary closely regulated by the 'net value added,' which allows for the extra responsibility and quality of the work.   Scarcity value drives the offers for such posts well above the rewards for those tasks for which the supply is regular, and high enough to attract the ability required, but it hardly ever touches the limit of productivity. Above these minima, special prices will be offered for reputed extra ability.   The size of a business in relation to others where high remuneration is given means that its top salaries must bear comparison with them.   There are, therefore, lower limits set by the necessity for clearing, by a quite definite margin, the levels of salaries in the same business which have a comparative basis.   Such a basis may be said to exist for comparable positions up to £3,000 or £4,000 per annum.   And the higher executive who has several such posts under him would certainly secure £5,000, in a vertical comparison. But there are also horizontal comparisons, and the board of a company with a capital of £10,000,000 might well feel they ought to pay

[1] This term has a special significance in economic writings.   In general it means the net difference made in the total product by the last unit employed.

their head executive rather more than was known
to be paid to the head executive of a business
with a capital of £500,000. Above this, no
rules or standards apply, save those comparisons
with the managing owners of private business,
for reasonable consistency at this point is also
expected. Moreover, at this higher stage the
weight of taxation at 10s. to 12s. in the £ is not
without its influence on the gross salary, for an
addition of £1,000 gross means only £400 net in
spending power, and that may be an insufficient
incentive for greater responsibility in some cases.

But, although it may be demonstrable that
such men are worth their money and the community ought not to grudge it, it is quite likely
that they would work just as hard for much less
in a community where lower salaries were the
rule, where success in life was not judged by the
levels reached, and where they were not serving
large masses of capital interests. The ' game
of business,' the free exercise of decision and
power, and public esteem, would go far to make
substituted incentives, once the whole idea had
changed. We are considering, not how little
the community can pay them for the much
greater values which the community enjoys by
their efforts, nor whether it is ethical for the
community to expect them to go on giving back
the surplus, but whether their efforts would be
forthcoming actually on some different basis.
We may compare the security and the dignity of

Civil Service positions which reconcile the holders to salaries considerably below what might be necessary in ordinary business life.   The officials are, in fact, rarely required to produce a *profit result*, and that test does not apply ; there may be many in a particular grade who could not do much better for themselves under competitive conditions, but there are certainly a few who could command salaries four or five times as great as can be obtained in their particular grade.   The stimulus of reputation for efficiency and some sign of recognition is equal in its incentive quality to very large additions to salary. The loss of pension rights is a very substantial barrier to a change of career, at the time when the necessary ability has been demonstrated.

Professor Paul Douglas, after examining the biographical material, gave an analysis of the non-economic incentives as follows : (1) a desire to benefit humanity ; (2) fascination or joy of the work itself ; (3) desire to project one's own personality into the work ; (4) desire to be esteemed by one's fellows in the same field ; (5) a desire for the esteem and approval of the general public ; (6) a craving for notoriety ; (7) a desire for power over man and over things.[1]

PUBLIC SERVICE

The enormous amount of work that is done on public bodies of all kinds, in local and central

[1] *The Trend of Economics*, pp. 153 *et seq.*

government, for nothing but the love of the work
or the esteem of the people, indicate the presence,
especially in Britain, of a large and reliable fund
of non-economic incentive.   How far is this ex-
tensible into other fields ?

Before assuming that there can be a considerable transfer of the important work that is done
gratuitously to-day into a different sphere, one
must remember that much of it may be done by
those who have a sufficient subsistence in other
ways.   They might not be so willing to work for
non-economic rewards if they had not this background.   Moreover, where the large percentage
of all service is given for a cash reward, there is a
distinction in giving public service for no reward
at all.   It cannot be said that, in a field in which
there is *no* specific monetary reward at all, this
same distinction would remain, and, where
everyone is actually or compulsorily altruistic,
the general level of work so performed might
be far lower than where altruism derives its
hedonic satisfactions from its comparative rarity.
McCurdy says that the phrase ' every man has
his price ' is intended to be cynical.   Yet it is a
proof of existing altruism.   It shows that some
considerable margin of compulsion or attrac-
tion is necessary before a man will sacrifice either
loyalty or conscience.   Much depends on how
greatly the group action can seize the imagination, for a group formation can certainly increase
loyalties, as we can see in every society or

association to which we belong. In a large number of cases they exact a higher standard of conduct than the individual life alone would render. McCurdy says, ' The group that cannot exact sacrifices from its members is moribund, if not already disintegrated.' Not every group is of this order. ' The best example of a selfishly motivated group is that of the shareholders in a large company who retain their shares so long as dividends are forthcoming. But among even these are apt to be directors who develop pride in the business as such and complicate their operations with loyalties.'[1]

It is said that a Japanese delegation were asked to report on the basis and incentive of public service in England. They reported that they found many of the ablest men would work very hard for long periods, and, as a result, have a piece of ribbon given them and the right to put several letters of the alphabet after their names, and that, strange as it might seem, they seemed to be quite satisfied with this culmination to their efforts. I have often heard Americans, taken off their guard as true democrats superior to such distinctions, regret that they had no system of ' honours ' in public life which would be worthy objects of ambition and clear signs of proved worth, but at the same time they were never confident that such a system could be properly and honestly administered.

[1] *Mind and Money.*

There are certain activities in our modern society in which we find, and expect to find, financial incentives least active, and in which the usual alternatives of social prestige are also unimportant. The calling of a minister of religion is, by its nature, ' other-worldly ' in its motive. When a reasonable subsistence has been provided, there is no thought that differential ability or effort should be attracted by higher pay. Only those who are thoroughly acquainted with clerical psychology can say how far this formal aspect is subjectively perfect. There are in most denominations modest ranges of emolument within which ambition or desire may operate. Men like to succeed and to be appreciated, and, in so far as gravitation of the abler or more popular to the better paid positions is an outward sign of approval and success, the differential may act just as it would in commerce. Cases of men deliberately choosing for non-personal reasons a lower paid position, when the higher is open to them, occur, but are not numerous. In the Church of England, ' calls,' or preferment to new livings, are nearly always upward in emolument, and in the Free Churches a similar movement is observable. But men do not work less or more conscientiously through these differences. A legitimate desire to deal with family responsibilities adequately is a sufficient incentive to change, without bringing in the purely personal factor. The profession is sacrificial as a whole, for a number would obviously have done better for themselves, by their gifts, in worldly reward in other professions. The young man cannot always tell; the older ones in many cases cannot be judged on comparable lines, for their habit of life in the calling has unfitted them for direct transfer, and the ' might have been ' is difficult to judge. But quite obviously some who are particularly fitted for pulpit work would never have earned more in open competition in other vocations than they are now getting. Whatever the facts may be the social way of looking at it is that it is a profession which demands sacrifice, and therefore, psychologically to the individual, it must do so. Perhaps the ideal case is where the ' call ' is so powerful that the man is unconscious of sacrifice—the real pain would be for the call to be denied him. But it is a little more real, and helpful, if the sacrifice is severely felt at the outset, and then forgotten and merged in the calling—a little more human, too, if it occasionally returns and there is a hankering after the fleshpots. James Chalmers said, ' Don't send us fellows who talk of self-sacrifice.'[1] If the sense of sacrifice is constant, then the call must be spurious and ' verily they have their reward ' is not dominant. In the mission-field the ' call ' may have been helped in the past by a sense of the heroic, of danger, of adventure, or

[1] Oman, *Concerning the Ministry.*

change and wanderlust, of a desire to do the most
difficult thing.   But when once on the mission-
field, often prosaic, drudging, and unappreciated,
these factors are not so sustaining.   It is the
nearest to pure self-sacrifice that this order can
give us, and we reverence it without cavil or
derogation from its quality.

Next, the medical profession is ranked as
calling for a sense of personal sacrifice and
risk, and to some extent it deserves the distinction. Much work is done for nothing at all,
and professional pride commands that it be done
just as well, but of course the power to make
highly differential demands on people who ' can
afford it,' which exists equally in no other profession, must be brought into the balance, so that
in the end the average income may bear comparison favourably with that accruing to similar
skill and devotion elsewhere. If there were
equal distribution of incomes, the methods of
remuneration in the medical profession would
have to undergo a drastic change. It cannot
fairly be said that financial incentives are
unimportant. Other professions, such as the
solicitors, architects, and accountants, have
recognized scales of fees, by agreement or
convention, and the scope for the financial
incentive is really similar to that of piecework
in industry, though personal mastery is more
dominant. Barristers have a high differential
' rent ' of popularity, and therefore power to

GM

discriminate against the purses of wealthy clients or cases where large sums are involved.

We have to come to the field of invention and science to reach another set of incentives. If these could not exist in a different order, the consequences would be particularly serious to the standard of economic life therein.

It is interesting to look at the motives of great scientists : Faraday, although connected for some time with commerce, and getting an increasing income, came to the conclusion that he had to make a choice, and he put it deliberately aside. But then he was very exceptional. Even the honourable non-economic rewards given by his peers did not influence him. When he was offered the presidency of the Royal Society, he said, ' If I accepted, I would not answer for the integrity of my intellect for a single year.' We should not have many Faradays, even in a translated sphere.

The work of Clerk-Maxwell and Darwin and Wallace, of an altruistic kind, cannot be divorced from the fact that they enjoyed private incomes. The simplicity of Pasteur and perhaps of Metchnikoff, and Huxley's long fight to work along scientific lines without reference to monetary rewards, are important cases for study. On the other hand, Agassiz was not really swayed by any desire to benefit mankind or posterity. Vanity, even to the point of lack of scruple, was his clearly marked motive, and Sir Humphry Davy's

life does not show him as always actuated by
motives of the most excellent order.   There were
those like Kelvin, Edison, Perkin, Parsons, and
Van Siemens, who made money freely with their
scientific discoveries, and cannot really be invoked to prove the point we have at issue.   More
interesting, perhaps, is the case of Newton, who
ceased to be really creative and productive after he
secured safety and salary in his office at the
Mint.

The truth is that in the field of invention
and innovation the motives are mainly non-
commercial—the joy of the game, the lottery of
success; these throw up amid countless casualties
those intrinsic successes which are invaluable to
the next rank of less enterprising *entrepreneurs*.
When the risks are proved and output is steady
it becomes the subject of successful communal
exploitation as a third stage.

How much of social progress is due to these
various elements is not strictly determinable.
We need to have knowledge on a more definite
and scientific basis about the strength of desire,
and the extent to which it prevails, to do a
workmanlike and efficient piece of work ; of
man's ability to sacrifice for a principle, for an
institution or for a person ; and of his craving
for recognition by others.   It has often been
held that the classical school of economists
minimized these factors.   Exactly how powerful
are they at the present time ?   Or to what extent

can they be cultivated and made the mainsprings of action ? We want an examination of the actual cases, similar to that which William James carried through in his *Varieties of Religious Experience*. It is true that most of his examples were rather of the abnormal type, and that, while they may prove inductively, beyond all scientific dispute, that the factor of religious experience is a reality and a great power where it occurs, in the right type of individuals, they do not tell a great deal about the strength of this force in the average man or mass of men taken together. In the same way, the examination of particular instances of altruistic economic life might be deceptive if we took it as representing what the man in the street was prepared to do.

Says one writer, ' The trend of society is to emphasize the acquisitive qualities. Money is necessary, not only for survival, but for power and, in a large part, for public respect as well. The motives of working for the sake of the work, for altruism, and for non-financial recognition find themselves swimming against the swift-flowing stream of financial pressure.' Certainly the incentives of captains of industry—the men whose minds and powers we should rely upon for progress in a new state of affairs—can be reduced to economic terms in the majority of cases. We are bound to say that any evidence of non-economic incentive that is obvious in business to-day cannot be taken as final, if we try to estimate the possible strength of a non-economic motive in a different environment.

It was said by Henry Ford of the true captain of industry: ' He is an instrument of society, and he can serve society only as he manages his enterprise so as to turn over to the public an increasingly better product at an ever-decreasing price, and, at the same time, to pay all those who have a hand in his business an ever-increasing wage based upon the work they do. In this way, and in this way alone, can a manufacturer justify his existence.'[1]

Harriman said, ' I never cared for money except as power for work. What I most enjoy is the power of creation.' It may thus very well be said that power and not profit is the primary fascination. If a similar place can be found for this incentive in a new state of affairs, there may be no great change in their output. The leader of a wholesale co-operative society, getting only £400 a year, remarked, ' I enjoy the respect of my colleagues, and I possess great power. These things satisfy me.' The question has been put, ' Do not able men demand such high salaries and monetary rewards under capitalism in large part because they feel the chief rewards under capitalism are but money ? ' In this country we have a much greater spirit of public service than in many countries abroad. If you were to tell

[1] *My Life and Work.*

an American in many States that a man is prepared to spend much time and effort in a certain activity *for its own sake*, you would simply not be believed. Here we find that to do a thing for a small sum or for nothing may, in itself, be a distinction, and a subject of pride. Service on committees, on the judicial bench, by scientists, by all who have a sense of ' calling,' may be far more on the non-economic plane than general economic activity.

We need to examine ' public spirit ' a little more closely. It may hide many different motives, and be just as hedonic or self-regarding as profit. For, after the first needs and early vanities which purchasing power can satisfy have been met, men often want the prestige of unselfishness, or of the ability to work for nothing. ' Inverted egoism ' accounts for a good deal of public service. Although the motive for the doer may be no higher, it can, of course, be urged that payment by praise or position costs the community nothing, and to that extent is more economical than money reward. Whatever may be the man's motive for unpaid service, many would say, ' Let us take advantage of it for the common good. It costs us nothing and pleases him. The machine works with the cheapest fuel.' But, while this may be a popular view, it is not an instructed ethical one. After a long and detailed consideration of mixed motives, especially that passion for

approval which is ' essentially a puerile incentive, needful to elicit the energy and sustain the
courage of schoolboys, soldiers, and sailors,'
Dr. James Martineau said that the pompous
professions of its historic variety by grave
seniors before applauding senates are humiliating
indications of how far we still are from the moral
manhood of the human race. He concluded
significantly, ' For a vast proportion of its
computed gains from this source, society pays
too dear in the degradation of minds capable
of action from better springs.'[1]

Service on local councils may not always be
self-sacrificial, and many motives of self-satis-
faction may enter into it. I have not enough
knowledge of it to say how far a sense of power
and importance is dominant, but a brief experience as a charter mayor gave me a little insight into the motives at work amongst men of
real parts, and certainly public gratitude to them
is not conspicuous. ' I've been in your ward for
twelve years and you've never once been round
to ask for my vote,' was said by a lady to a district councillor. ' I've served as your councillor
for twelve years and you've never once been
round to thank me for my services,' was the
quick and just retort.

The point of all this study of human motive
which preachers and teachers, whose field of

---

[1] *Types of Ethical Theory,* Vol. II., Bk. i., on ' Idiopsychological
Ethics,' p. 242.

action is human motive, should explore, and be thoroughly acquainted with, is to consider how far non-financial incentive is capable of being substituted for financial, and how far such existing motives will work as well, or better, in a different order. Those non-financial incentives which consist in the distinction of public service might cease to act if such service became common form contributed by all. But, *ipso facto*, the work would get done, and perhaps, in place of the present distinction of doing it for nothing, there would be an avoidance of the stigma of not living up to the average public performance. There would perhaps be a wider spirit of emulation to do unpaid public work better. But transfer of motives to a new order might mean that the wide range of responsible public work at present done by leisured people with private means would have to be paid for. In many ways the number of absolutely ' unearned incomes ' at the present time is not as great as we suppose. I am not in a position to judge how far much unpaid committee and council work is indispensable, and how far it is a mere façade for the work, and even decisions, of the paid technical expert, secretary, clerk, and accountant. Certain it is that the best amateur commission or committee is often completely dependent upon good technical whole-time *expertise*. Again, even the amateur, unpaid official is not always an unmixed blessing, and many a committee or board of a charity or public concern has longed for a paid official who will be conferring no favour by his work, who can be brought under discipline, and be actually expected to contribute the quality of service for which he is paid.   Unpaid work is often dearest.

On the whole, I incline to the view that there is no substantial obstacle to a higher order ultimately, from the point of view of productivity, because of the non-transferability of motive and incentive in this particular field of service. There is already in existence a splendid body of semi-altruistic motive to act as a nucleus in an order making great demands on public spirit.[1]

BUSINESS PROFITS

Now we come to the wider field of economic activity known as business, productive and distributive, avowedly animated by the ' profit motive.' There are several sub-divisions : small one-man concerns ; larger private concerns under ' captains of industry ' and financed by private capital ; public companies with salaried heads, and relatively private capital, with unquoted shares ; large public concerns with publicly subscribed capital in shares easily bought and sold on the stock exchange by holders having no interest in or knowledge of the businesses and their personnel ; co-operative

[1] On the whole subject see H. G. Wells's *The Work, Wealth, and Happiness of Mankind*—viii. ' Why People Work.'

societies ; municipal trading. In all of these there is a competitive element.

The question of the motives that operate to produce savings from the individual, and accumulate ' capital ' for general use, is too vast for treatment here. Large though the assumption may be, it will be assumed that the more Christian order we are postulating will be sufficiently productive, and appropriately managed, to produce collectively, or otherwise, the capital necessary for its progress and development. Nor can we examine the form of directorial management through boards ' responsible ' to shareholders, as the saying is. Even within the present order much could be suggested in American, British, and Continental types which would be more ethical and perhaps of great practical significance where there is a conflict between the interests of the concerns themselves and the interests of the larger community.[1]

We must proceed direct to profit as a motive in a competitive régime.

The term ' profit motive ' is fast obtaining a complex of unworthiness, which is probably justified for only a small fraction of the different ideas that are comprised and confused under it. In economics, profit is used in two senses : one a normal return for service, necessary to evoke the supply of that service and to keep it maintained ; and the other a surplus (arising on part

[1] *Vide* p. 40.

of the supply of an economic good) due to the existence of certain advantages which that part of the supply possesses over the remainder. Now the first kind of profit attaches to business activities, chiefly, for the people who take the initiative in bringing the three inevitable part-ners together : labour, capital, and management. The initiator usually takes the residual risks of diminished reward or loss. If a set of workmen started a venture, they would make calculations as to the cost of the capital and supervision, and expect to have a margin on sales at least equal to the wages they could get. But, though their motive might be a wage, it would, nevertheless, be the speculative element. Similarly, a land-owner might hire his capital and labour, and calculate to make a balance on his accounts at least equal to what a tenant would pay him. This ' rent ' would be the ' uncertain residue.' The usual procedure is that in which wages and and and superintendence are taken at market rates, and the reward of capital is made the uncertain variable. But these three forms of initiative might all refer to the same enterprise. In one sense the enterprise is " for " the remuneration of the initiating party, because it is the initiator, but it must first, or in its stride, be for a gross income, which includes the remuneration of all the parties, out of which that of the employed parties has priority.'[1]

[1] MacGregor, *Enterprise and Purpose and Profit*.

Thus, if there is anything wicked about profit
it seems to be wicked to be the initiator or risk
taker. In a similar way we can imagine a man
with £500 savings thinking of employing himsel
and them in running a small shop, and he wil
expect to make at least the wage he would get
from a store company, plus the interest he would
receive from putting that money in a savings
bank. Yet what he actually gets is called
' profit,' and he is actuated by the profit motive
Profits in this sense are partly earnings o
management or personal labour and partly in
terest on capital, and if he could not get them he
would not go into business. Profits of this
kind are differentially loaded for special risk, or
exhaustion of capital, in each case the profit
being required to evoke the supply. J. R. Bel
lerby goes so far as to consider that the employ
ment of one group by another may be the result
originally, of differences in the ' capacity to
sense the future. It may be but the Parable of
the Wise and Foolish Virgins writ large.'

Now the slogan ' Production for use and no
for profit ' does not get rid of these elements
it only smothers them up, and it assumes tha
only one type of economic activity instead o
each of them is working for its ' earnings.' But
the second kind of profit in economics is of a
different order. Suppose that the total supply
of a particular product is 1,000,000 units
marketed at £1 each, the out-of-pocket cost

eing 18s. for all but one concern—then every
ne makes 2s. per unit profit in the first sense.
uppose that they are all the same distance from
he consuming market and transport costs 2s.
er unit, except for concern A, which is much
loser, where transport costs only 1s. per unit.
oncern A makes 2s. profit in the first sense, and
ets an extra 1s. (there being only one market
rice possible at that centre) as a profit in
he second sense, a surplus due to advantage—
the little something the others haven't got '—
nd the advantage here is proximity.   This is an
conomic ' rent,' and such rents may arise by
ll kinds of advantages—extra productivity,
ewer machinery, lower rates, and managing
bility superior to the average. Now, unless all
roduction proceeds under identical conditions,
hich is impossible, these differentials must
ctually exist, whatever we call them, and
hatever the form of industry. The main
uestion is what we do with them. In indi-
idualistic industry they go to the initiator.
hey are the profit motive, and cause him to
earch out for the lowest costs everywhere he
an, and the search on a wider scale causes
ndustry as a whole to take the best positions,
nd thus all costs are reduced to the common
dvantage. Sometimes large differentials exist,
nd stand for a good time before they are worn
own by others, and these are the cases to which
he obloquy of the term ' profit motive ' most

applies. Someone is always making such surplus of advantage, but it is rarely the sam person for long.

There is very little permanence about thi economic or surplus profit unless there is monopoly or franchise. In a competitive régim profits shift from one unit to another in a su prising way. The time curve of high and lo profits in the aggregate may be of a certain typ and be stable, but the position of individua businesses on that curve is continually changin This has received important statistical verifica tion in the researches of Professor Secrist.[1] Th existence of the surplus is, in fact, inherent in price system.

We are familiar with the conditions unde which a greater reward, i.e. a higher pric stimulates a greater supply, and a less rewar brings about a smaller supply, inasmuch as i the short period, at any rate, owing to th principle of diminishing utility in the satisfactio of people's wants, the greater supply cann command a continually higher price. There is balancing mechanism brought about throug price which is at the very foundation of economi life, and is the final deciding factor of the way i which men's efforts are distributed betwee alternative walks of life. There are sometim exceptions to this general rule of a temporary c particular character, e.g. a very large outpu

[1] *The Triumph of Mediocrity in Business.*

may be deliberately marketed, not in response to a higher price, but with a specifically lower price —foreseeing that the increase in supply itself would enable a lower unit cost to be secured, the producer is exploring the *social demand curve* to find the new position of equilibrium for a larger quantity at a lower price. Again, whereas a falling price ordinarily checks supply, in such a case recently as American farm produce it has had the reverse effect. If the farm were heavily mortgaged, its charges had to be met, and the owner argued that, at the lower price, he must sell substantially more in order to make up the fixed charge upon him, so that low prices positively brought about even larger increases of supply than high prices would have done. But these are merely back-washes of the very general principle of regulation by price.

A first essential then, is to decide whether we shall use ' profit ' in its economic sense, as a differential surplus, which must really exist all the time, whatever the form of economic society, so long as the factors of production are unequal in their productivity, and whatever name we may give to it. There is a common price of all supply—even in a Communism that has no open price, its place is taken by a marginal cost— which yields that part of the supply having any advantages over the other parts, a surplus. The advantages may be in location of raw materials relative to manufacture, or of both to the point of convenient use; in efficiency of labour management or machinery; in some elements of luck. The determining limit is at a margin where wages of capital and management and interest just meet and just evoke that supply in continuity. The superior advantage of a unit gives it a profit. A continual struggle is going on, not so much between the different factors as between competing units in the same factor, to search out positions of this advantage and secure this surplus. Human behaviour in reaction to the search for this particular 'profit' is a different study from that which follows a normal reward or profit necessary to evoke and maintain normal effort, which is found at the margin where the other profit is non-existent. The chance of making the economic surplus through seizing and holding some advantage in production has acted as an immense incentive to risk-taking and enterprise—something that it is very difficult to replace. This great element of backing one's own judgement may have an element of the lottery, but it has prompted many adventures. But the great point is that the surplus element cannot be got out of the system. It might be appropriated by taxation, theoretically,[1] and the benefit given to the community, as advocated by J. A. Hobson, but the practical difficulties are insuperable. We should then leave 'normal profit' as the remaining economic

---

[1] *Vide* my *Principles of Taxation.*

incentive, and, deprived of the *chance* of un-
usual gains, it might well be that this normal
rate, necessary to evoke the supply and maintain it, must accordingly be somewhat higher.

It is impossible to deal here with all the con-
fusions of thought attached to the idea of profit.
Apart from the elements which represent interest
on capital and wages of management, the element
for, or as a result of, risk-taking is an economic
inevitability. (*a*) ' The distinction so often made
between production for use and production for
profit is only the distinction between producing
for a known and producing for an anticipated
demand. . . . So long as there is an element of
uncertainty in the supplying of demand, there
must be profit.'[1] I would also add that so long
as there is uncertainty in the demanding of
supplies, there must be profit. By depriving the
consumer of all *spontaneous* liberty of choice or
change of choice, and by producing all supplies on
uniform terms—only by these two devices can the
differential surpluses called profit be eliminated.

The marginal productivity of a man's labour,
which is one of the limiting determinants of
reward in a complex community, may be justly
due to him and must be granted to him if he
consciously insists upon it, but the question
whether it is economically essential to secure his
services, and whether he *needs* the result of his
labour, is a complex theoretical question which

---

[1] Lindsay, op. cit., p. 93.

Hm

admits of no simple answer.[1]   Clearly in the case
of higher executives, and professional services,
it is not always necessary.   So far as the mass of
workers are concerned, the question more often
raised is the sharing of profit.   Now a business
with a particular advantage (to which the worker
in it has contributed nothing) will make a profit
surplus, while another which has no such
advantage will make none.   The workers in
each may be equal in ability and energy, and by
hypothesis their wages are also equal.   Why
should one set enjoy an uncovenanted advantage
or surplus remuneration which the others do not
possess ?   There is no reason in equity, save that
it may be better that some workers should share
the surplus rather than none.   It would seem
that, so far as the needs of the community and
the accidents of situation, &c., and not superior
management or foresight are the source of
differential surplus, that surplus should be spread
over the community as a whole, and not go for-
tuitously to particular bodies of workers.   So
long as business is conducted in independent
units, this is impossible, and there seems to be
nothing obviously more Christian about this
particular type of incentive to wage earners than
others.   Profit sharing may be too much of a
lottery for that.

Those important classes in an ordinary capitalist régime, who are risking their own capital

---

[1] *Vide* R. F. Harrod, *Economic Journal*, March 1936.

with their own management, produce many trials, a large number of failures, and a few successes. If one reviews the early commercial history of artificial silk, or of flying, or of the Zipp fastener, and sees the extent to which risks were taken and capital invested on evidence and calculations which would not satisfy any rigid tests, one is driven to ask whether any committee would be willing to risk public money for which it would be answerable on a similar basis. Committees are always ready to decide, when conditions are proved and when comparisons can be made to indicate the possibility of success, but they must inevitably play for safety, particularly as, by the nature of the case, the successes will tend to be far fewer than the failures. The one who plays for safety can get a reputation for wisdom because his successes exceed his failures, but, even so, his absolute number of successes may be fewer than that of another person who, while having a majority of failures, attempts more. A committee responsible for public money might, perhaps, be prepared to do the same if they were given a fund specifically for trying out invention and new ideas, but without any questions being asked, and only subject to an audited probity.

J. R. Bellerby avoids much of the difficulty by substituting for the expression ' profit motive ' the term ' self-interest,' and his analysis of what this includes is the basis of his constructive scheme for a contributive society. Needs of the body, hunger, sex, and the senses, make up ' natural ' self-interest. ' Acquired ' self-interest is mental in origin, and includes all consciousness of self, viz. improvement of status, and appreciations of various kinds. ' Group self-interest ' is usually regarded as virtuous, but ' if its aim is merely to pool the interests of its members, the self-interest that emerges is no more virtuous than the self-interest of each individual member.' Wars give a test case. In industry the group-interest of the family is the strongest factor. His analysis shows clearly that self-interest is not in itself bad, but only where it proceeds to extremes and produces hurtful results, by ' destroying harmony.' Indeed, the expression of the individuality inherent in self-interest is an essential feature in economic progress. He asserts also that a certain degree of private property is necessary to the same end, although this right leads to many of the worst results of the economic system[1] : ' the vanities of display, the emergence of class distinctions, gross inequalities in wealth, industrial leadership selected on the basis of inheritance, and the setting of false standards of social obligation.' The sacrifice of a part of a comfortable surplus is wrongly hailed by many as ' generosity '; which shows our false philosophy of possession. Amongst the virtues of property he cites its unique power to symbolize ; thus

[1] Op. cit., p. 55.

a souvenir in private hands has untold value in actualizing the values and experience of life. ' A well chosen gift may be the only possible embassy of an inner thought—even the destruction of something owned, a cask of ointment, may have a meaning for which there is no other method of expression.' There is a practical point: The only person who really respects any piece of property, as it should be respected, is he who has the travail of producing it. Spenders of the earnings of others tend to become extravagant.[1]

The motives attached to production as an activity include the aspect of it as a competitive game.[2] Many praise it as such, but others see in the way the cards are dealt a source of real social discontent. Professor Knight says inequality in the enjoyment of the product is less important, as a source of opposition to the system, than the far greater inequality in the distribution of economic power, opportunity, and prestige.[3] Modern literature on incentive is largely devoted to keeping the game interesting. The functions of the game and the want-satisfying agency are inseparable, but in ideals incompatible—one means distribution according to effort ; the other the ' tools to those who can use them.' His searching analysis, to which we are all

[1] Op. cit., p. 59.

[2] J. R. Bellerby classifies competition as a ' habit of conduct,' at present in some confused balance with co-operation as the essential of business.   But he distinguishes carefully between ' *acts* of competition ' and the ' *spirit* of competition.'

[3] *The Ethics of Competition*, p. 60.

much indebted, shows that, unlike most games, the effects of success and failure in one round are progressive into the succeeding rounds. He goes perhaps rather far in saying that a fascinating sport for the leaders has been *made so by reducing it* to mechanical drudgery for the rank and file.

We sometimes talk as though only in this age have we become alive to the abuse of business motives in competition, or the desire to analyse them. But the noble-minded economist, Alfred Marshall, father of the modern science, nearly fifty years ago[1] analysed them in terms which could be used to-day. His headings are illuminating. ' The love of money is only one among many '—' instincts of the chase '—' money as the proof of success '—' economic progress requires as a condition free individual responsibility, but not the maintenance of those rights of property which lead to extreme inequalities of wealth '—' the Socialists have underrated the difficulty of business work '—' public opinion of growing importance as an economic force—it needs to be educated for its responsibilities,' and so on. Thirty years ago he returned to the subject of economic chivalry, in which he held that (1) progress is in the long run *delayed* by exaggeration of the evils inherent in present economic conditions, and (2) that social disaster would probably result from the full development of the collectivist programme, unless the nature

[1] Presidential Address, Section F, British Association, Leeds.

of man has first been saturated with economic chivalry. He held the view that human nature is ' not yet far enough improved away from its primitive barbarity, selfishness and sloth, to be ready for any movement in this direction so rapid and far reaching as to effect with safety any great increase in wealth by a mere redistribution of material wealth.'[1]

' The behaviour of the community is largely dominated by the business mind. A great society is a society in which its men of business think greatly of their functions. Low thoughts mean low behaviour, and after a brief orgy of exploitation, low behaviour means a descending standard of life.'[2]

THE CENTRAL QUESTIONS

When I ask myself whether the existing motives will work a planned society—and so many identify a more Christian order with the abolition of competition, which involves planning on a national scale—I reply that the answer to the question put does not depend to a major extent upon moral values, or ethical betterments.

(1) Man is so constituted that he cannot help the diminishing sense of satisfaction received from successive increments of enjoyment. This will stand in any environment and it leads to the ceaseless, silent principle of substitution. This

---

[1] *Memorials*, pp. 323 *et seq.* and p. 366.
[2] W. B. Donham, *Business Adrift*.

leads to the phenomena of price tests as correctives of over- and under-supply. How price and interest are to be measured in a planned society is still unsolved from an economic point of view.

(2) It may not be said positively that output *cannot* be secured in the mass without the forces of fear, self-interest, and self-preservation, or without being responsive to degrees of reward. But the probabilities of other incentives working so well, with less than the educative environment of some generations, is certainly small. The physical laws of fatigue and human interest are *prima facie* against the idea that an extra hour's work can be dissociated from a differential stimulus. This leads, with the physical facts about capital goods, to a supply curve of costs, also inescapable. This again means that the planner has a double task, on both sides rather against human nature.

(3) I do not despair of the spear-head of progress and invention being thrust, in a planned society, into unconquered knowledge. And the communal control of it in capital application will be less wasteful of capital, but it will also be less advantageous in the net balance of gain in a given space of time.

(4) I think a community isolated from world economy must be lower in its economic standard. How to relate the planned community to an unplanned world, without introducing such

elements into the plan as to rob it of its planned character, has never yet been worked out.   How to plan a world economy without destroying the better elements of nationalism is beyond our examination at present.

(5) From (2) must follow the existence of differential surpluses or units, in either state of society. The economic aim of the planner should be to reduce these; the political temptation will be to maintain and appropriate them for other ends.

My provisional answer is, therefore, over a major part of the field, ' No '; over a certain smaller but important part, possibly ' Yes,' and over yet a balance of the area probably ' Yes.' But I have only exposed a part of the mechanism to view, and more attention ought to be devoted to the psychology of the plannees alongside of elaborate study of plans and planners.   If existing motives will not work a more Christian order because that is a planned order, the next question is : Are different motives really available ? And the third is : Will Christian motives be the kind involved ? I conclude this section by a word in appreciation of the present order.

Individualistic capitalism and the competitive system have been and still are a rich soil in which wheat and tares both flourish. The evils and abuses, economic and moral, are immense, but the fine features are numerous too.   And, whatever the world may come to, it will have been an essential experience, and its growth, apparently so irreligious, is strangely rooted in virtues at one time supremely acclaimed by religion. In the Middle |Ages religion ran economic productivity underground. The immense economic advance of the nineteenth century was the joint product of Calvin and James Watt. Their departed spirits worked in unconscious partnership to make the greatest business concern the world has ever known.

In an odd fragment of Alfred Marshall's writings[1] he thought it probable that a future social order would greatly surpass the present in justice and generosity and in the subordination of material possessions to human well-being; and even in the promptness of its adjustments to changing technical and social conditions. But he declared that we must always be grateful to the excellence of the work done by the present order, through free exchange, in turning to account the combative and predatory energy of the present crude nature of man, supplying the driving force which endowed crowded districts in the Western world with material comforts and intellectual training beyond those attained previously, even in places where Nature's bounty was larger relatively to the inhabitants. Gratitude to this now much-abused social order of the nineteenth century is overdue.

[1] *Memorials*, p. 367.

ADDENDUM TO CHAPTER II

Extract from ' Business as Social Service,' by Lawrence
Richardson (*Journal of the National Institute of
Industrial Psychology*, May 1936)

MOTIVES IN INDUSTRY

' It is often said that the motive should be service,
not gain, but this seems to me faulty psychology;
there are various other motives besides these two, and
the problem is not to set one in opposition to another,
but to get them all working harmoniously together.
I do not believe it is either possible or desirable to
eliminate the desire for self-advancement ; there would
be something very wrong with a family man who was
not anxious for the advancement of his children. What
we need is to make it clearer and surer that only by
serving the community can a person earn his livelihood
or secure advancement.

' The idea of service begins as loyalty to the business
unit, and this may be a powerful force. A typist, very
much torn as to whether she should accept a much
better place than anything we had to offer, said to me,
" I have worked here fifteen years and I feel as if the
business belonged to me." This sense of loyalty can
expand easily wherever there are personal relations,
e.g. to a trade union or employers' federation ; but
there is difficulty in its expanding widely, and often
from mere lack of knowledge it gives rise to a sectional
mass selfishness which may become dangerous. The
most dangerous development of all might be a national-
ized exporting trade if it failed in consideration for
other nations.

' The interest of the work itself, and the satisfaction
of trying to make a good job of it, is another strong
motive, and a great help in facing a disaster, such as a
fire or a breach of trust. In spite of much drudgery,

every good workman takes a pride in his work. A Scotch labourer with a specially greasy job said to one of my partners, " Aa love ma wurrk ; aa'm wrapped up in it." But it is undeniable that mass-production methods have taken much of the interest away from the rank and file and concentrated it in fewer hands ; there is some compensation in the reduction of toil and increased leisure for other interests. The use of machinery often demands a higher, not a lower, degree of intelligence.

' The desire for the good opinion of one's fellows is like the air we breathe, hardly perceptible, but influencing everything we say and do ; if allowed to dominate it may be disastrous ; in its proper place it is a valuable help in keeping us up to our best.

' All these four motives are present in a great variety of occupations. In addition, there may be others in special cases ; the search for beauty for the designer ; the urge to know in all research ; the maternal instinct for the teacher. A few people have a strongly developed desire to manage others ; a most valuable quality as long as it is united with wisdom, and so long as too many others do not share it. We need to have the help of all these motives, and to have them working as a harmonious team. But certainly the more the motive of service can dominate, provided it has a wide vision, the better for every one, and certainly for the employer's peace of mind.

' A business life is full of difficulties, worries, disappointments, mistakes. The competitive atmosphere is not easy. One has to be on guard, too, against fraud and sharp practice. But business could not be carried on at all unless most people were trustworthy ; no nation can be commercially great without a high standard of honesty. Business is interesting, and a great many of its relations are pleasant. For those who have the opportunity, it is a calling well worth the best they can give it.'

CHAPTER III

THE EXAMINATION OF THE CHRISTIAN MOTIVE

LIMITATIONS OF TEXTUAL AUTHORITY

WHEN we are desiring to base a social or economic order upon the Christian ethic, we have to ascertain, of course, what that ethic really is, and actually teaches, so far as it relates to the economic life. Hundreds of volumes have been written upon this theme, and the most diverse systems and practices have found their support from the New Testament. The cynic will say that we find what we are looking for. At any rate, we have reluctantly to admit that there is no universally accepted body of doctrine with a clear and unequivocal economic or social bearing.

Two things at least are, however, practically common ground. First, that no system or programme was laid down in the New Testament, applicable alike to the first century and the twentieth, to the primitive community, or to the advanced. Democratic self-government, for example, is not prescribed. If Christ had outlined a system, it would have been outgrown and superseded many times. So much is admitted even by the Rev. Stanley Jones,[1] who is the most dogmatic and definite writer of recent years upon the economic meaning of Christ's teaching. Second, that nothing of any value can be based upon specific isolated texts. No time will be wasted, therefore, in pursuing these two aspects.

But there still lingers a desire to base theories upon a collection or collocation of texts. A theory is elaborated, and around each point appropriate ' dicta ' are hung or arranged with no regard to valuations in their economic context, their apocalyptic outlook, and susceptibility to generalization from the particular.

How many texts are disqualified as guides to the life of to-day on the ground of their limit of outlook, I should not like to estimate. The Greeks and Jews had hardly the faintest idea of development or continuous progress and adaptation as a characteristic of society, and that its adjustments would become the central problem. The tempo of change was so slow, and the communication of its results so imperfect, that it was hardly perceptible. As Dean Inge says: ' In many of our social problems we cannot find the help in the Gospels which we should have welcomed, because the early Christians never thought about an earthly future for the human

---

[1] The author of the well-known work *The Christ of the Indian Road* in his *Christ and Communism*.

race.'[1] The exact limitations of the actual texts through apocalyptic and eschatological conceptions are naturally matters of opinion, and there is no received body of opinion. Hirst claims that the injunctions to watchfulness and business diligence ' in view of the early return of the landlord,' about laying up treasure, and the hard sayings about family ties, riches, and non-resistance are not contingent upon them, but are ' intrinsic and essential.'[2]

I place as much stress upon the absence of (a) international responsibilities, (b) biological conceptions of heredity and responsibility to the future, (c) a sense of natural development and ' progress,' when considering New Testament ethics *sub specie aeternitatis*.

DIFFERENT INTERPRETATIONS

Some find that the many conflicting interpretations of Christianity preclude their introduction into a scientific discussion. But they all agree that it is hard to make the Christian conception of goodness compatible with competition.[3] For the last was to be first. In a real sense, however, he who would be chief should be the servant of all, and many a chief business executive has no higher, or indeed no lower, ideal. The Greek looked at the character of the result, the beauty or perfection ; the Christian

[1] *Christian Ethics and Modern Problems*, p. 57.
[2] Op. cit., p. 72.   [3] Hirst, op. cit., p. 35.

at the motive and its spirituality. It is true that correct perception of goodness satisfied the Greek, whereas conscientiousness in doing what one imagines to be right is superior in Christianity, but this does not absolve the Christian teacher from the search for the absolute right, a search which is progressive and never final.[1]

' Morality, once an undoubted possession of mankind, has come to be a difficult problem ; instead of ruling over man from the height of its superiority, it seems now to depend on his opinion and choice.'[2]

Psychology carries on where ethics used to stop short, and both ' happiness ' and ' sacrifice ' get merged in a confusion which is almost metaphysical. The logical dilemma in ethics is whether ' altruism ' has any meaning. To do the unselfish act gives us ultimately more of the higher satisfaction than to be selfish; therefore we still ' please ourselves,' but in another way that benefits others. ' For a man to dispense with his own advantage for the good of others . . . by this means a good man finds as much pleasure one way, as he parts with in another.'[3] Then, again, to be indifferent to well-being and good things, in a stoic sense, or even in the application of the principle of not taking thought, by some ascetic Christians, is to

[1] On this, see especially Percy Gardner's *Evolution in Christian Ethics*.
[2] Eucken, *Present Day Ethics*, p. 33.
[3] More's *Utopia*.

deprive unselfishness of its value, for if we do not value the thing of which we deny ourselves for others, where is the virtue ? But I prefer to revert to the plain man's natural view that sacrifice does exist, and cannot be argued away. My Dr. Johnson would kick the stone here too.

Critics of Christian teaching therefore say that it is riddled with the ' profit motive ' or reward incentive.[1] The sacrifices we are asked to make in distribution to the poor, loving enemies, giving up family life for Christ, are all to be more than balanced by treasure in heaven, up to a hundredfold. The evangelical appeal of the nineteenth century was full of avoidance of eternal pain or of rising to everlasting bliss as a completely sound hedonic investment in the long run. And we know how social reformers accuse the Churches of applying religion as a ' dope ' to keep people content in that station in which they find themselves. These various quotations we might counter by others without any such incentive.

LIMITATIONS IN APPLICABILITY

Fifty years ago it would have been sacrilege to have suggested that the teaching of the New

---

[1] I have passed rather easily from ' motive ' to ' incentive,' whereas if this were a book on ethics as such, I should have drawn a careful distinction, but I think no practical difficulty will arise. My earliest mentor in ethics, the Rev. A. E. Balch, defines a motive as ' a desire transformed into a practical incentive to action ' (*Introduction to the Study of Christian Ethics*, p. 43). My own practical distinction is that in ' motive ' the emphasis is on being *pushed* towards the objective, and in incentive on being *pulled* by it.

IM

Testament was not, when interpreted, a complete guide to modern social conduct. To-day, its complete inadequacy is recognized by most careful thinkers, though even scholars so used to the traditional view sometimes slip into the old language. For example, a great authority described it recently as ' a treasure house of principles that admit of application to all the circumstances through which a Christian can possibly be called to pass.'[1] Dean Inge says we must continually remind ourselves that the standard in the Gospels is not ' a code of permissible conduct for a large community,' but throughout his work he holds society closely to the exampled principles of Christ.[2] Canon Barry in his great work, *The Relevance of Christianity*, deals most frankly with the relation between the moral teaching of Jesus and the Christian ethic. ' For the old-fashioned believer, and perhaps still for most modern Englishmen, the recorded sayings of Jesus are to be revered as infallible guides to right living, were we but brave enough to carry them out. . . . There are, among the sayings, injunctions which, if obeyed literally by all who seek to be loyal followers, must prove definitely incompatible with the continuance of society.'[3] He proceeds to give a masterly summary of the nature of this ' obsolete bibliolatry,' and by the contradictions

---

[1] *Methodist Recorder*, April 16, 1936.
[2] *Christian Ethics and Modern Problems*, p. 67.
[3] Op. cit., pp. 70-1.

alone he shows how particular sayings must have been addressed to particular conditions, fatal to the ' glib notion ' that the moral teaching of Jesus is, as it stands, sufficient guide for problems of conduct and the perplexities of the modern age. He speaks helpfully to the younger generation, who have been taught to expect this universality of application and find that ' two-thirds of their ethical questions seem to be, not merely unmentioned, but not even contemplated in His teaching.'[1]

TEXTUAL PROOF

The method of proof by agglomerated texts, generally treating each as of equal value and disregarding their differences of background, date and provenance, reached its climax, for economic and social conduct, in the seventeenth century. Baxter was the most reasonable and enlightened exponent of it, but the most remarkable example I know is *The Husband's Authority Unvail'd* ; ' wherein it is moderately discussed whether it be fit or lawfull for a *good man* to beat his *bad Wife*, a subject to some, perhaps, as unwelcome as uncoth. From an inner Cloyster of the Temple, by Moses a Vauts, a faithfull Votary, and free Denizen of the Common-wealth of Israel. 1650.' Here the rather smuggish, humble author proves, by the

[1] Op. cit., p. 76.

aid of many hundreds of scriptural texts, his thesis in favour of wife-beating, provided the husband is reasonably virtuous and his wife unreasonably incorrigible. ' If the Tongue of a *Clamorous Woman* be allowed to walke at large, a Man may be brought to such an Exigent ; that he shall not have a quiet Corner in his own House or Heart to retire himself unto, for Prayer or any Exercise of Piety ; but be forced out into the Fields, Woods, or Caves (a seemly sight for a Man to over-run his own House and Wife, is this the *Wifes reverencing her Husband* ?) least his humiliation (as Davids) be both inter-rupted and reproached : there being some Woman (a sad Thing to consider) who, though conversant in Scripture, do, yet, abhor their Husbands under the Notion of Piety, or (as they say) preciseness ; and would be apt to insult the more fiercely, upon any damp or visible dejection of spirit in them.' Also, ' But, if *they* will needs *forget* themselves to be *Wives*, their *Husbands* must yet *remember* they are so : If they be so insulse and impudent, as to vilify, affront and defy their Husband (under that Notion especially) That is, if they will be so *willingly* grossly *ignorant*, as not to know their *Head* from their *Feet*, they must be satisfied with Fare suitable to their Manners, not their Means or Mannors : for, how can they in reason claim so copious an Alimony, or kind Usage, if they scorn or scant their Husband of that

Authority afterward, which God gave and themselves granted him, at First.   Or, if they make no
dainty to strike at their *Head* (though but in
Word onely, they have heard it wounds deeply)
they must not disdain a little scratch on their
Body, or to be deplum'd of a little Pride by their
discreet and conscientious *Husband* for their
good.   I beleeve the direfull Martyrdom of but
a Member of the Lambs beloved Wife before
described, is sowrer Sawce than 1000 dry Blows
(or if a little bloody) bestowed on some of our
coy, cross, domineering Dames.   In short, if
they cannot or will not cary, in some degree,
conformable to the Prescript and Patern of that
Weaker Vessell set them down as moulded and
framed by the holy Ghost ; they must permit
their Husband, in some proportion, to exercise
that knowledge and coactive power which God
hath imparted to him, while not contradicted,
but commended by his revealed Word : That,
after they *have suffered a while* for their Faults
or Folly, *they may glorify God their day of Visita-
tion* ; and (at last) with their Fellow Servants
and just Sufferers, have all *Teares wiped away
from their* eyes.'

THE TESTS OF TEXTS BY INCLUSIVENESS AND WORKABILITY

We are not even to-day wholly free from
occasional attempts at proof by collocation.

But on the whole we can say that a more reasonable selection is made and harmonized by most writers. It is common ground that we must seek for the underlying principle and then elaborate it. Now I would lay down two working propositions: (1) Any principle or theory of ethical intent for social application should take into account *all* the available material, and either reconcile every part of it, or be a very high common factor of it. Any ' exception that proves the rule '—i.e. strains it to the point of doubt—must be kept seriously in view, to be accounted for in the synthesis so far as possible. (2) Objective applications of principle so derived must be tested by their ability to ' work ' in practice. They are not necessarily to be the most productive economically—for we must not fall into the common error of supposing that the more ethical must *necessarily* be the more productive[1]—but they must keep the economic machine at work, and keep it in stability, sufficient to give a minimum of subsistence to the population. Those principles that will not ' work ' must be referred back for re-examination of the premises. Of two alternative interpretations that one is to be preferred which most successfully co-operates with Nature for a high standard of life.

On the question of ' inclusiveness,' I have often been put to some difficulty because I have

---

[1] *Vide* my *Christian Ethic as an Economic Factor.*

not been able to see at once whether an imposing array of textual support is complete, or only selected. In forming my own judgement, I have found the necessity for a rather confused search over the ground. In order to reduce this difficulty, I have for my own purposes constructed a complete ' Economic Canon of the New Testament ' by taking out all material that in my judgement can have any really relevant bearing on man's behaviour in the production, exchange, and distribution of wealth and his relative regard for it. By a rough classification of this material, I thus get, in one view, so to speak, without further search on particular occasions, all that the New Testament has to say on economic problems, undisturbed and undistracted by other matters which, however important spiritually, cannot be brought on to this plane. I thus simplify the mechanics, if not the intellectual problem, of inclusiveness, and, as I am not aware that this has ever been done before, I put it into an Appendix for others to use,[1] in the hope that it may serve a useful purpose and save them the trouble and risks of specific searches. It has, of course, the obvious disadvantage that it is a *personal* arrangement, and others might have different tests of relevance.

[1] I do not suggest that some others have not been strictly inclusive in their survey before arriving at their conclusions, but they have not exhibited the data with quite this visual assistance, and one is unable to judge. Dr. Ryder Smith, in his *Bible Doctrine of Wealth and Work*, obviously came very near to it, but several prominent issues to-day were not challenging questions when that was written.

No two people would draw the line in exactly the same place.

It is no part of the purpose of this Lecture to make a complete induction of Christian ethics from this material, exhibiting the whole process. It must suffice if I state a few particular conclusions of my own, and refer to other and differing inferences, in the attempt to answer the question : What is, in fact, the Christian doctrine, if any definite doctrine exists, at certain crucial points ?

THE POSSESSION OF PROPERTY

There is no essential condemnation of a property system. It is assumed to be essential, and is worth trouble and care to get and preserve. The idea of property is more obviously assumed for personal consumable wealth, but property in productive assets is not excluded. Expropriation is not supported, but the moral responsibilities of possession are great, to individuals. There is little guidance on social or collective responsibilities. The injunction to sell, and distribute, seems to be for application to individual lives for spiritual reasons ; it is not easily capable of generalization into a basis of economic society. For, if one sells, others must buy. All cannot be sellers. Pearls of great price and alabaster boxes of costly ointment cannot be disposed of at all in those types of equality which are usually assumed in an egalitarian community.

The Existence of Wealth

Rich people are not intrinsically wicked by the possession of more than others ; but by their attitude of mind towards their possessions.[1] In the use of income the claims of the poverty of one comes before those of the superfluity of another, but this is not a basis of industrial remuneration nor a premium on idleness. It does not test what is due to a man, but what he does with what is due.

The Existence of Poverty

References to ' the poor ' sometimes must mean the *economically* poor, at others the poor ' in spirit.' It is a matter for argument whether Christ envisaged any time when there would not be any ' poor ' economically. In any case we are in difficulties, because poverty is a highly relative term, and what would be a good standard of life in a country in one age is abject poverty in a succeeding one, or what is a fair standard at a particular time in one country— and in full accord with the possibilities of that country—is a standard of destitution at that same time in another. There is nothing in the

[1] ' We say that wealth has undue power to-day, but its greatest tyranny is over the possessor.' (Lee, *Social Implications of Christianity*, p. 57.)

New Testament to indicate (*a*) that the world must be identically productive per man unit at all places in it, (*b*) that inequality of production must be made good by *collective* sacrifice of wealth between areas and nations, or (*c*) personal social responsibility for relieving ' destitution ' goes beyond what is ' in sight ' in time and place. Yet these three questions lie at the root of modern world problems. I incline strongly to the view that Jesus did *not* envisage the total abolition of relative inequality, but accepted some measure of it in the light of His knowledge of the time. Much of His reference to the poor did not touch the economic position. I know that this is not universally accepted. The good tidings which was to be preached to the poor was not, in the opinion of some, the spiritual Kingdom of Heaven, merely, but a social revolution which should abolish their economic poverty. Stanley Jones says that to put ' to preach good tidings to the [spiritually] poor ' is to take an easy way out from facing its ' plain implications.' He asserts definitely that the actual poor must be intended. And the ' good tidings ' is not spiritual news—it is not a promise of future reward, but of release from ' poverty,' not relative inequality. To get this conclusion, Mr. Jones claims to look at the passages ' bearing on the matter.' In these he does *not* include Matt. v. 3, ' Blessed are the poor in spirit, for theirs is the Kingdom of God,' which seems to

be a fair comment on the good tidings to the
poor (even if St. Luke's form is possibly more
authentic). But he takes Mary's song—the revolutionary[1] promise of scattering the proud, putting
down princes, exalting those of low degree, filling
the hungry, and sending the rich empty away.
The new Kingdom has as its first concern that
' poverty should be banished by providing for
the poor the good things which God has provided
for all.'[2]   It seems to me that Jesus accepted
the main social and political framework of His
day, and did not incite to revolution, although
Stanley Jones puts a superstructure upon
' release to the captives ' of ' emancipation for
the socially and politically disinherited.'   I find
no trace of democratic self-government, or other
similar heritage of such ' release,' and cannot
confuse his ' smashing of the priestly system '
with it ; nor do I feel that ' exalting them of low
degree ' is a programme of cancelling privileges
of birth and standing.   Then comes what he
rather strangely calls ' John's message ' of
every valley being filled, and every mountain
and hill being brought low.   This is taken to
mean that all must be ' shared on an equal
basis,' the depressed portions of humanity

---

[1] ' It has long caused me amusement to see a wealthy congregation
singing the Magnificat, which is much more violent than the " Red
Flag " '—Dean Inge, *The Social Teaching of the Church* (1930).
Also Canon Sheppard, *The Impatience of a Parson*, p. 146 (1927):
' much more revolutionary.'   This epigrammatic antithesis is useful
but must not be examined too closely.

[2] Jones, op. cit., p. 56.

are to be raised and the exalted brought down. He reinforced this with his condition of repentance in the sharing of two coats ; and so proved that he really meant, by mountains being brought low, an economic sharing. I cannot follow him further, except to say that he deals with the possible objections to this inference which might arise from the tribute to Caesar, and soldiers being content with their wages.

Let us provisionally accept the hypothesis, and apply my second, or realistic, test. It will not be contested that, whether the message was to the twentieth century or not, it was certainly uttered to the first century and intended for the poor of its time. If it was a spiritual message, they had it and could realize it, and many did so. If it was an economic promise, they never actually got it. The good tidings were not really delivered—they were a fraud. But *could* they have been implemented, in fact ? Even if the rich had given up not merely their surplus, but had gone economically (not spiritually) *empty* away—a rather unfair proceeding, and creating a new set of poor—would the resultant change in the condition of the poor have been such as to constitute ' good tidings ' ? If there is one thing quite certain about the economic condition of Palestine it is that the total wealth was such that an equal division would have left everyone still poor, judged even by their standards, and the poor were numerous enough, and the rich few enough, for the difference in standard on redistribution to have been almost imperceptible. Mr. Jones shares a very common delusion as to the extent of the economic satisfaction to be derived from equal division, from ' levelling mountains.' It is, and always has been, negligible as an abolition of poverty,[1] whatever it may do for the sense of justice or equality. Fifty years' progress in the arts and sciences is worth far more to the ' poor,' retaining all the inequalities in comparison with the rich, than any redistribution could possibly have been at any time of which we have statistical records. On the static plane, Mr. Jones's test would fail to-day, but it fails egregiously in the age for which the text-data were uttered. One most penetrating foreign critic, André Siegfried, thinks the English in particular are obsessed with the distributional panacea. ' The masses are concerned mainly with getting possession of a greater proportion of the national wealth which they are to possess. They take no interest in increasing or preserving that wealth.'[2] Nor on the dynamic plane, in wealth production, is Mr. Jones much happier when he says, ' The creation of one over-rich man usually means the sending of a whole host below the poverty line.'[3] It may be unfair, or unfortunate, or inequitable, but the fact is the two movements are not causally

---

[1] See my *Christian Ethic* for further details.
[2] *England's Crisis*, p. 150.   [3] Op. cit., p. 58.

related in this way in the productive process. The host are not made poor *because* he is made rich ; generally they are better off in the process than they would have been otherwise. This does not touch the quite separate question whether, this result having come about, the effects should be offset by a compulsory, voluntary, or social redistribution, in the interests of equity. I do not feel that Mr. Stanley Jones makes out his case for his interpretation, because (*a*) he has not used all the data, and (*b*) his result does not ' work.'

How different is Mr. Hirst's comment on ' Blessed are the poor in spirit '—' Not all can be wise in the Greek sense, but all can be humble in the Christian sense.'[1] He goes to the opposite extreme.

If we regard the wealth to be spread as homogeneously consistent, the statistical possibility of abolishing poverty is negligible enough. But qualitative limitation is severer still. You could not relieve poverty of this kind by sharing costly boxes, pearls, and the other impedimenta of the wealthy – these are ' wealth ' only to the rich, and their extra possession of food, appropriate shelter, and the simple necessities of life would be a very limited quantity, quite incapable of raising large numbers from destitution. The greater part of the ' value ' of the objects of wealth disappears when there are no wealthy

[1] Op. cit., p. 48.

people. They must be sold, for money, to other wealthy people, and the proceeds distributed, the money being used to buy, or produce, ordinary consumable foods.

Then, apart from the statistical delusions of quantity and quality, there is the fallacy of composition in this conception, viz. because a thing is feasible in all units separately, it is feasible for the whole. Because any rich man's pearl or possession can be sold, and the proceeds distributed, it does not follow that all rich men's possessions can be. There are no buyers.

Mr. Jones, indeed, has a vague awareness of the quantitative difficulty, but he only skirts it when he says that a library can be enjoyed in common, and the redistribution of this kind of surplus for common use would ' raise the cultural level by collective projects.' How does a diamond, at which all may gaze, fill the stomachs of the destitute ?

The general principle of improving the lot of the poor by reducing the wealth of the rich has so far not touched the productive side.

Sharing Wealth and Giving Wealth

In such questions as the sharing of wealth, there is all the difference between that process carried on as *to* the individual (and before he receives), or as *from* the individual, and after he receives it.   The latter derives all the virtues that

the Christian ethic gives it from the fact that
it is voluntary and not prescribed. If society
is based on every man *having* to make contributions of a certain order, there is little
ethical value left in the personal act. When
Mr. Stanley Baldwin gave up £100,000 of his
fortune for the national good, it was a fine and
great gesture. But every super-tax payer of
£100,000 is not entitled to a heavenly mansion
thereby. Moreover, all like being generous, but
not when it is expected of us. The fine, careless
rapture of giving by the widow who cast in ' all
she had,' which so exceeded the rich contributions, might have offended Aristotle's sense of
balance.[1] Equally it is defective as a motive
force for any economic organization, and derives
its value from running counter or ' extra ' to the
ordinary, being unorthodox and devoted. If the
case comes up for inclusion in a Christian order,
we are entitled to assume that the widow was
not dependent on alms the following day, but
had a means of livelihood or expectation of
income of some kind. Otherwise the trans-
action *as a basis for an economic rule* is difficult
to follow through realistically.

The moment we take the more equitable
sharing of wealth into the production field, we
lead into two important and related subjects :
' equal reward ' and ' payment according to
need.' Here more suggestive material exists.

[1] *Vide* Hirst, p. 62.

PARABLES OF REWARD

How many thousands of words must have been written about the ' parables of reward ' ! The literal observance of contract with the early labourers, and the free bounty to those who worked far less for no fault of their own, have been forced into every mould of meaning and principle. They extend from those who hold that a spiritual principle of reward in the Kingdom of Heaven is alone intended, where no nice equation of service and recompense exists, to those who see in it a principle of universal economic application in remuneration of effort— a kind of payment by need and not by effort. Stanley Jones sees : (1) The unemployed having more sympathy than the employed—their needs had gone on even though they did not work ; (2) a living wage independent of work, and unemployment insurance ; (3) that God wills equality. These things, he thinks, will not work in a competitive order, so Jesus Christ implied a co-operative order in which they could be found. The other workers, he says, objected, and this shows that inequalities do not depend on the will of God, but on the will of man. On this elaborate analysis, it is worth observing : (1) The owner was evidently short of workers, and if the additional ones had been present at the beginning they would have all been employed through the day ; (2) they turned up from

KM

somewhere else, during the day. There is nothing to show that *all* the unemployed were finally taken on. By a parity of reasoning, even those who were not employed for even five minutes might have received a penny. The doctrine of ' to each according to his need ' is certainly quite consistent with this parable, but it does not seem to me to be enjoined by it.

I agree very closely with Dr. Ryder Smith's view of this parable.[1] On the assumption that every one has done his utmost, and put in all he can do, according to his ability, in a perfect society, ' need ' is by far the best criterion of division.

But on a realistic test, of workability, much depends on the size and character of the society. For a small self-contained unit there is a *prima facie* feasibility in a common stock. But there is no way of making production equal natural demand, for to put in what you think you are best at, earnestly and conscientiously, may be to supply many things that are not wanted to the same extent—they do not enter equally into the needs of people. There is likely to be a shortage of things that ' need ' would really connote, and a surplus of things not included in need. A clear central direction of the forces of production would be necessary to get an aggregate supply suitable to meet aggregate needs—

[1] *Bible Doctrine of Wealth and Work,* p. 162.

for we have now put aside, by hypothesis, price-
tests of relative demand. But what is the meaning of aggregate ' need ' ? Need is a relative
term, truly subjective, and must differ amongst
persons according to the intensity of their feelings
—it is not a fixed thing, capable of aggregation,
and then of allotment. It must vary with total
production. In other words, the total production
is the fact with all priority. For example, let one
million units of most varied products come into
being, to be shared by ten thousand people—
their ' needs ' are not 100 units *each*, for that
assumes all men to be alike. Even if they were
alike, their needs might be 120 units each.
' According to need ' cannot mean more than
this : whatever the total production proves to
be should be shared out in *the ratio* of respective
individual need. It may give all of them
personally more than their absolute need, or
less. ' Need ' is, of course, an entirely expan-
sible, flexible idea, as we see if we look at the
standard of life in this country over a hundred
years, or look at the standard of a Japanese
agricultural labourer against our own, or a
factory worker there, in Bombay, or in Lanca-
shire. But are we quite sure that ' in the ratio
of need ' is just ? Need proceeds in a fairly fixed
order from physical up to mental and cultural
elements. The total need of two individuals,
A and B, might even be identical at 100 units
each, made up in A's case of $80x + 20y$ (x being

physical elements and y non-physical) and in B's case of $40x + 60y$. Now suppose that portioning out total supply only gave 80 per cent of what they ought to have or ' need.' Strictly applied, this would give 80 units each; $64x + 16y$ to A, and $32x + 48y$ to B. But this might reduce B to a skeleton. If you introduce the money element, certain difficulties creep in; and, without it, I have tried in vain to establish a quantitative criterion for division according to need. Dr. Ryder Smith says: ' In a perfect world there would be a common stock in some form or other, to which every man would, of course, contribute his utmost, and from which he would—equally of course—draw at his need.' This to me frankly jumps every difficulty, and I do not see how we can make practical aims towards a perfect world without facing some of them.

If all this is the case with a simple society, what can we say of a world of States, bound together by exchange, but free from rigid isolationism and nationalism? I can get no effective stopping-point short of an international world State, with complete equality between its parts, however unequal their racial ability or local productivity, and with fluid migration breaking up racial settlement. We may assume that the Hindu or Hottentot would contribute much as he does now, but I am not clear how his ' need ' would be assessed as against that of a European. Nor do I know how the central direction of

production and of allotment which is postulated
is to be made effective.

Long and earnestly have I tried to conceive
the practical way of making the supposed
principle of the Vineyard (which, after all, was
likened to the *Kingdom of Heaven*) work an
economic society in a temperate zone, with a
dense population, in such wise that it can be
made an immediate goal of policy, in the
enviably facile way that writers like Mr. Stanley
Jones are able to do. But I have tried without
success.

I take refuge in a resolve to use the principle
of ' need ' to the utmost in social security, relative taxation, and personal relationships. But
I believe the poor will get a better standard of
life actually by a system in which some inequality on this principle prevails, than by one
in which short-sighted effort for the closest
equality to the principle keeps down to a lower
level the total production available.

There are grave and inexcusable inequalities
in modern life which have *no functional value*
economically in inducing maximum production,
and which have a fatally baneful influence upon
men's minds and souls—nearly as bad for the
' too muches ' as for the ' too littles.' They are
not as grave as they once were. But our eternal
vigilance is necessary to keep inequality down
to that which has functional advantage. In
a really imperfect world, unconscious of its

imperfection, men may rest content with differences of reward and desert. In a really perfect world—i.e. of perfect people—they would not worry about inequalities, for selflessness would prevail and jealousy be absent, so that ' the little more and how much it is ' would be irrelevant. It is only in a world passing from one to the other that we make so much of it.

The fact is the Parable of the Vineyard leads much more directly into ' equal reward ' than into ' payment according to need.' But equal reward must be tested as a New Testament principle, in the light of other equally important material. Canon Barry says quite bluntly that we cannot look to this parable for light on the conditions of modern industry, the minimum wage demand, or the rights and duties of employers.[1]

The Parable of the Talents illustrates differences of ability and responsibility, and apparently advocates differences of reward, for there is no indication that the three servants became recipients of the seven earned talents equally between them, or of any proportion. The unfruitful one talent in stock was paid over to the ablest man, apparently for his own reward, and not for reinvestment for his master, otherwise the conclusion ' to every one that hath shall be given,' &c., loses its meaning. Certainly the ' one-talent man ' was not paid

[1] Op. cit., p. 72.

' according to need,' but there was a general principle of reward according to ability, *or* opportunity, *or* faithfulness. One inclines to the view that the two- and five-talent men were equal in ability, and might have been equally successful if their opportunity had been reversed, although it is open to argument that the five-talent business represents higher managing ability. The distribution of opportunity itself was a little fortuitous. Stanley Jones finds here ' *from* each according to his ability,' and no support for differential reward.

E. W. Hirst concludes that the Parables of Reward show that the wages of virtue are the ' wages of going on ' to larger spheres of service. ' The idea of reward is out of place suggesting as it does the conception of merit. The Vineyard Parable implies that we do not really *earn* anything at God's hands.'[1]

My own conclusion is that differential rewards ought certainly to be *earned* by differential stewardship, and possibly by differential ability. An economic order which involves this is not inconsistent with the parable, but a co-operative order in which there is equality of reward for differential service is also compatible but not enjoined.

Judged by the realistic test, it cannot be said that it would be *impossible* to work a productive community on this principle, if differential

[1] Op. cit., p. 103.

incentive is not essential, and we are left to judge this immediate and ultimate objective on the widest evidence.

Some Economic Aspects of Equal Reward

In further consideration, therefore, let us develop the realistic side in its economic bearings. We are apt to look upon this question of equal reward from the supply side. One shovel is like another, and commands the same price, irrespective of whether it is produced by a slow or a fast worker. No one suggests that the consumer shall vary his offer for it according to the difference between a poor and a good workman, or a lazy or an industrious one, and, so long as the producer's difference comes out in a time-quantity relation, the consumer is indifferent to it. If the producers work direct for the consumers, this differential comes out inexorably— one man gets a great deal more for an hour's labour than another, or, put another way, one earns much more in a day, if he wishes to, than the other. But interpose an organization— which greatly multiplies the total productivity of labour—a supplier of capital, or a manager, and the principle seems to many people to change, and, if it is equal pay for unequal product, but equal time, it is deemed 'more Christian.' Even if the organization passes on the gross price received, as it might well do in a co-operation of individual workers for one market—' the whole produce of labour ' to the labourer—it can only do so by an average reward, which produces quite a different result from that reached by individuals working separately.

But we ought to check up the principle of equality on the demand side in other directions too.   In the case of direct services, no attention to industry or worthiness can get rid of innate or acquired differences of skill.   We cannot stop thousands flocking to see Alex James play ' soccer,' Perry tennis, or Obolenski as wing three-quarter, where only hundreds go to see Smith or Jones ;   we cannot prevent the box office ringing with cash for a film in which Grace Moore is singing, where another house is showing a poor story to an empty house.   The populace are prepared to lay aside this basis for their popular favourites, just an inch or an ounce or a semitone better than equally hardworking and ' deserving ' colleagues, letting them get an enormous remuneration that might make a great general or scientist or Prime Minister green with envy if he judged life by money.   The rent of notoriety for the popular idol is enormous, and there would be much indignation if some managing syndicate or middleman got in between the box office and the idol and intercepted too much of it.   A remuneration which for an industrial leader of the workers' livelihood would be regarded as monstrous and ' ungentlemanly '[1] is conceded ungrudgingly to the leader of leisure. Under a planned economy on the egalitarian principle, all artists would receive the same remuneration, and the incentive to do their best would come in the larger drawing-power, and the testimony of a crowded house would be the effective reward. To what extent the planned economy would recognize the right of the neglected or less popular singer, or actor, or pugilist to continue his pursuit and draw his equal pay, or on what principle he would be required to change his profession, is not easily seen. But it is obvious that, from the demand side, the ' consumers'' liberty to prefer one producer to another throws a great strain on the practicability of equal pay as a working principle. For greater talent creates its own rent, whether it receives it or not, and it is not easy to distribute that surplus fairly to marginal producers just on the verge of being accused of not being fit earners at all.

There is a further complication on the supply side. One supremely competent artiste, or player, can ' supply ' or entertain thousands just as well as he can hundreds—with no more effort. But a supremely good surgeon cannot. Even if all his potential customers had equal incomes, some would be ready to forgo more than others for his services and pay relatively high fees.

[1] Cf. Tawney's *Acquisitive Society*.

The consumers' competition among themselves would give him a rent of ability. And something would have to be done with that rent, the balance being paid presumably to the neglected surgeons. Some would get over this by instituting a table of fees, like a lawyer's, applicable to all practitioners, on the hypothesis that any one of them is equal to any other. The favourite surgeon would then find that he had twice as many operations to perform as his indifferently endowed colleague. The next step, to cancel out the vagaries of patients' choice, would be to ration the work, and order that all the practitioners should have an equal number of cases, and so earn an equal standard reward. This would be ' dragooning the patients,' indeed.

Bellerby supports co-ownership as the means of redressing inequality of wealth, but he does not deal with this problem of comparative results and of losses.

OTHER ASPECTS OF EQUALITY

Many escape the difficulties of ' equal monetary reward ' by considering other forms of equality of a more ethical character. These considerations are so numerous and diverse as to be outside our scope.

The emphasis of modern Christian ethics to distinguish it from all other types is the equality of brotherhood and all that is derived from it, and this goes much further than ordinary material equality. But exactly how to use this idea in the production, as distinct from the consumption, of wealth is not very clear. Some find it in equality of opportunity, but differ as to the extent of the opportunity. The Platonic view of equality of opportunity stopped at education. The differences that persisted were the very stuff of his organization of society. Education and selective breeding made the ideal man. But, to-day, equality of opportunity is carried much further as an idea, for it precludes inheritance of wealth, though it cannot preclude inheritance of ability. Nor is it agreed that equality of opportunity of all material kinds carries us as far as equality of inner satisfaction. It is not possible to equalize enjoyment, even if we equalize the opportunities for it, by opening parks and galleries and State operas to all. For, just as men vary greatly in what they can contribute to the common good, so they differ in what they can obtain from it. Worldly and financial inequalities seem bad enough, but they are nothing to the spiritual and intellectual inequalities. Fortunately, they occasionally offset each other. It is well recognized ethically that you cannot realize or equalize community in ' goodwill.'

E. W. Hirst insists that, even when you have made opportunities equal, the individuals may remain apart, even hostile.[1] ' Any quantitative

[1] Op. cit., p. 130.

ideal for well-being is bound to be ill-fitting and unsuitable.   Nor is such an ideal an inference from the Christian ethic.   It is the *unity*, rather than the equality, of men for which Christianity stands, and this ideal of unity demands, not equality, but rather *equity* of opportunity.'

By every route examined we reach the result that equality in provision for man gives no sure basis for a perfect or Christian society without a high development of character and self-abnegation. ' The self-realization of the Christian is essentially based on self-sacrifice—which is the sacrifice, not merely of this pleasure or that, but of the self as an object of independent and self-sufficient worth.'   He ' dies to himself.'[1]

When we have passed from equal reward or equality of various kinds, we have reached the rival concept of varying reward, which in its ethical content is ' *reward according to need* '— often treated as if it were the same as equal reward.[2]   Writers upon distribution ' according to need ' generally mean by that phrase what is *necessary* to man, but they often slip inadvertently into the thought or quasi-synonym ' want,' meaning what a man *desires* to have. These are two radically different conceptions, and, in the literature of ethics, psychology, and

[1] Op. cit., p. 113.
[2] ' The Soviet slogan is " From each according to his ability and to each according to his needs," which is, and must always be, the opposite of equality in sharing.'—Lord Passfield (Sidney Webb) in *International Affairs*, 1936, p. 405.

economics, there are many shades of meaning and classifications in each. We seem when studying them to be engaged in a highly academic and unpractical exercise, but, as a matter of fact, if these differences get into our practical suggestions for the division of economic product in a better order, they work devastating confusion in thought. If we are trying to divide the economic product of society according to real need, with the yardstick of calories, vocational necessities, and all the paraphernalia of direct assessment of that need, and in particular in relation to the place which a particular individual is called upon to occupy in the organization, we may be far from satisfying his natural wants, as judged by himself. The allotment of cigarettes, drinks, books, songs, both ' necessities ' and ' luxuries,' viewed from need and from want respectively, must differ very widely according to our leaning towards the purity of one extreme or the other, according to our conceptions of liberty, of happiness, or even of the ends of life.

The Problem of Values

I do not propose to deal with the fine distinctions between different types or degrees of desires, except so far as they are relevant to the main subject of this Lecture, as bringing significant differences in their effects on the production and distribution of those economic satisfactions which enter into a standard of life. Is production to proceed on the basis of what men actually think they want, or what some one— or even a majority—thinks they *ought* to want, because it is good for them ? A more perfect world is not going to be achieved by the more ethical distribution of entirely unethical values. Its perfection will consist quite as much in the better valuation of what man wants to be produced as it does in the rationale or mechanism of their distribution. Upon the first plane of values, those physical and elementary satisfactions which maintain or increase the power to produce and enjoy satisfactions of that, or a higher, order clearly present a problem of multifarious technical character in which the pulpit has no particular technique. But, once these are dealt with and we approach satisfactions of mental and spiritual appetites, we enter upon a sphere of values not to be judged by the apparatus of biochemists or industrial psychologists or humanist doctors, a sphere in which the minister should be, or strive to become, an expert. The Church should be the custodian of life's values and the exponent of the art of living, raising the standard of demand in the individual, so that, in course of time, what man needs and what he wants will be identical.

Nor is this so hopeless a task as might appear. Desires are the basis of motive for the force in the economic machine, analogous to motive power in physics, and they are consistent enough over a reasonable period to be used as a postulate. But average desire can be changed over a long period, both in itself, modifying the construction of the machine to its change. Wants, past the purely physical stage, grow and change. ' The chief thing which the common-sense individual actually wants is not satisfactions for the wants which he has, but more and better wants.'[1] ' Life is not fundamentally a striving for ends for satisfactions, but rather for bases for further striving.' The competitive system may well be the most productive in the aggregate. It may well leave the under-dog much better off than another system, more ethical, but less economically productive. But the inferiority of its by-product of ideals is the high price we pay for this economic advantage. We can try to rid the system of those by-products and keep its gains ; *or* we can take the risk of pouring away the material ' baby ' with the unwanted and un-ethical bath-water. ' Keeping up with the Joneses ' may be a stimulus to economic en-deavour, acute and persistent. It may even raise the dignity of life in some of its aspects, as much social emulation may do. But we associate far too much our enjoyment and our success in achievement with ' keeping up with or going ahead of other people in a rivalry for things about whose significance, beyond furnish-

[1] Knight, p. 22.

ing objectives for the competition itself, little question is asked.' One of the tasks of the Church, as the chief ethicizing agency, is to keep the Western world, in particular, alive to the fact that there are other sets of values, and that our best religious ideals do not square with those now predominant. ' Our modern civilization, bad as it seems in some respects, is being kept from corruption largely by the influence of Jesus on millions of lives in all the countries of the world.'[1]

Now one organization of society can call forth and nourish higher values than another. Much of the evil of a competitive system is made by the system, and the values that would be created by a more contributive or co-operative system would in many respects be higher ones, whether the output of material commodities proved to be more or less. But we cannot guarantee it, for the over-estimate of the importance of money, and the things which money will buy, may be as great among those who wish to redistribute wealth as among those who wish to maintain things as they are.[2] A great American professor of economics declares that there is no more important function of a first course in economics than to make the student see that the whole problem of social management is a *value* problem, that mechanical

---

[1] Hirst, op. cit., p. 130.
[2] Cf. Inge, *Social Teaching of the Church*.

LM

or technical efficiency is a meaningless combination of words.[1] Far indeed is this from the conception of economics which limits its activities to the mechanics of motives and efforts regardless of their content. He would judge the existing order more by its value standards than its efficiency in producing the values demanded. ' The economic order does far more than select and compare wants for exchangeable goods and services : its activity extends to the formation and radical transformation, if not to the outright creation, of the wants themselves ; they as well as the means of their gratification are largely products of the system.' No one with a sense of history will question the truth of this judgement, and it is small wonder that we crave new orders and systems with high essentials and potentials because we believe that only thus will men rise to nobler possibilities.

Certainly, there are three claims for the betterment of valuations : first, the individual in his own judgement of what life means ; second, the emulation and expectation created in the environment ; and, third, the nature of

---

[1] Knight, *Ethics of Competition*, p. 43. I greatly regret that I have to join the majority of writers in insisting upon distinctions under the vague term ' values,' now so overworked and the cloak of much loose thinking. Some day we shall re-analyse this term and find what lies beyond it. It is used in so many different senses, and puts ' finis ' to most open arguments. What does Santayana mean, for instance, when he says, ' Spiritual life is not a worship of " values," whether found in things or hypostatized into supernatural powers. It is the exact opposite ; it is *disintoxication* from their influence ' ? (*Platonism and the Spiritual Life.*)

the machine. Now the first is especially the preacher's opportunity in his personal appeal. The second is his duty, too, in his attitude to social conventions, to the aims of life, where the Church can, and must, take a lead ever forward. For the third, it is a serious responsibility for the Church to advocate changes in technical organization whose essential needs are pitched far beyond the average motives of the mass of men, for such a new order will be foredoomed to economic failure, born before its time. If the Church cannot show that it has brought the wills of men within hail of the new demands upon human character by its appeal and standards, it must be chary of giving promissory notes to social revolutions. But this is not to say that the Church cannot sponsor social betterment; far from it, and it should do so at the sacrifice of potential economic betterment, as it has done many times in the nineteenth century. For if the new demand is pitched at a point attained by a reasonable number of individuals— if it is not born before its time—the rest have an object-lesson and a goal. It may not be possible to make men moral or unselfish by Act of Parliament, but they can be given lessons and object-lessons in morality by it. And public enactment is a great educator. The rise and fall of the Prohibition movement in America should be worth examination from the standpoint of how far ahead of human character one can safely go. There is no power in the world like an idea whose time has come. As much judgement is wanted for that time as for the idea itself. The task of the Church under the third head, the ideal- and character-forming power of the machine itself, is obviously to support heartily all modifications of social compulsion which are well sponsored in a technical sense, and to prefer to win a little ground and consolidate it well for the next advance, than to make revolutionary changes in society. The considerations which are in point in dealing with the method of a new order have now to be reviewed.

CHAPTER IV

ON METHOD

WE have considered what motives and incentives at present animate men to economic activity; we have endeavoured to ascertain whether the Christian canon provides material for dogmatic assertion as to the motives and ethical ideas that can be feasibly employed to economic ends; we have agreed that the methods or systems employed may to some extent react by evoking and developing those very motives, not otherwise to be found active, which are necessary to such systems. We have suggested that the Christian teaching, so valuable in the realm of motive, gives little or no guidance upon system and method, and it is that most technical part of the field into which we now enter.

Is tariff policy essentially less or more Christian than freedom of trade?—democratic institutions more than benevolent dictatorships or Communism?—British parliamentary institutions more than the corporative State?—the gold standard than a tabular price standard?—proportional representation than two-party systems?—orthodox central banking policy than

Social Credit policy and Townsend schemes.
In these and many other controversies on
method and system, sides have sometimes been
taken on ethical grounds, and therefore, not far
away, on grounds alleged to represent Christian
principles.

Most of us would claim to judge by results.
But we must be called upon to judge ahead of
results by probabilities, because the trial cannot be made by experiment, and if we change
the system, and the expected results do not flow
we have gone from bad to worse and worked
material havoc. In this judgement of proba-
bility we have to consider to what extent any
social system consists of modifiable human
character, and how far it is made up of physical
arrangement and unmodifiable human necessity
and material objects.[2]

However important motive may be, it must
act in a material framework, and perhaps in all
such possible frameworks there are certain
common and inescapable features, whatever
we might wish otherwise.

ESSENTIALS OF ECONOMIC MECHANISM

Bellerby puts the methods or mechanisms in
this order: First, money, which is almost
essential for the exchange of goods, and the

[1] e.g. 'For the Christian, collectivism is a matter of expediency
rather than of principle' (H. G. Wood, op. cit., p. 70).

[2] *Vide* especially my *Christian Ethic as an Economic Factor*.

development of the principle of division of
labour. Second, from this, a price system,
which ensures that goods are produced in the
proportions which give the community, as a
whole, maximum satisfaction from its existing
labour and capital. Third, price inevitably
involves the profit system, and this provides a
means of eliminating the decadent part of industry, and rooting out the inefficient. Then the
fourth dependent principle is the wages system,
which ' permits the assessment of the cost of
different types of labour and so renders accurate
accounting possible.'[1]

All this seems to be preliminary to the introduction of differential motives for production,
or ideals of life, and it should be carefully
weighed as an irreducible minimum of environment given by a writer very critical of existing
conditions. But different money systems which
make different conditions for exchanging goods,
and therefore give different results in the actual
division of labour, may affect the consequential
' shape ' or operation of the price and wage
system. These differences, in turn, may con-
ceivably give one kind of motive a better chance
than others. So the machine and the motive
are always related. One system may make it
easier to do right and harder to do wrong than
the other. Hirst says that Christianity teaches
that the seat of morality is the motive, whose

[1] Op. cit., p. 82.

influence extends to its expression in act, and determines the character thereof. Favourable external conditions have only a derivative value ; they have no intrinsic goodness, but merely provide virtue with a better opportunity of expression.[1]

' Plato seems to think, as do some moderns, that, if you socialize possessions and institutions, you thereby socialize the wills of the members of the community. . . . The abolition of all private property and of family life will not cure such selfishness, which will surely break out in some form or other, whatever be the social and political arrangements of the State. . . . Jesus demands the regeneration of the soul rather than a socialization of institutions. The first need is a change of the human will : institutions will change as a result.'[2]

Graham Wallas did modern thought a great service which it has not yet absorbed, when he ' changed the focus,' as Lippmann put it, and turned political science away from the discussion of institutions, and no longer ignored the men who make them, and live under them. He turned the study of politics back to the humane tradition of Plato and Machiavelli, making man the centre of political investigation.[3] Dr. Link, an American psychologist, in a striking new work[4] declares that in modern trends there is an

[1] Op. cit., p. 60.   [2] Op. cit., p. 45.
[3] Cf. my tribute to Graham Wallas, in *Economica*, 1932, p. 399.
[4] *The Return to Religion.*

indifference to moral concepts, and that the tendency to look to mechanistic schemes, rather than to the integrity of the individual, really indicates a disturbing weakness both in ourselves and in our leaders. ' In our rediscovery of Jesus we find a far more profound thinker than the popular leaders of to-day. Christ was not a social reformer, he was a reformer of men.'

Bellerby develops with great force the thesis that the ' system ' is essentially character— human in every part.[1] Our habit of distinguishing it, regarding it as something independent, introduced from outside, leads us to miss its essential characteristic. It also leads us to miss seeing that alterations in the system involve alterations in collective individual habits. We ought always to ask the question, ' Can human nature rise to it ? ' I would add, ' If so, how soon ? ' But he certainly adds the dominating conclusion, describing it as of transcendent importance, ' No change in the structure of the economic system should be attempted which goes *radically* beyond the powers of human character,' and cites the failure to realize this in Russia. But he goes on to a logical inversion : to change the economic system *is* to change human character, and vice versa. Mussolini says, ' There is no revolution that can change the nature of man.'

How potent the system may be in limiting or

[1] Op. cit., p. 31.

developing character may be seen from the economic, non-ethical idea of division of labour, without which we could not keep a fifth of the population alive in decent comfort, and which at the same time gives rise to 90 per cent of our ethical problems.

Division of labour makes a situation in which the greatest acquisitions are to be made only through the greatest contributions. ' The more self-interested a man may be, the more he is driven to studying and satisfying the needs of the community. By this convenient paradox the economic system exploits self-interest to the full, turning it to the advantage of society as a whole. . . . By yet another paradox, it succeeds in placing power in the hands of those most intent on serving.'[1]

The system of division of labour is not dependent on only one kind of motive, it is clear, and some may be much better than others—it may evoke both types at the same time.

' The system tends to gain from all types of motive. The character of the motive seems to be of little account, in the material sense : provided it is cogent, the system will draw from it a full harvest.'[2]

THE DEFECTS OF THE COMPETITIVE SYSTEM

The system of competition we have already examined in the *motives* which it involves. It

---

[1] Op. cit., p. 80.   [2] Op. cit., p. 10.

is also possible to criticize it for poor economic distribution ; but more difficult to do so for its failure to produce. It has many defects even on economic grounds.

The power of pure individualism in competition to bring about an ideal utilization of social resources has been criticized by Professor Knight[1] on twelve classified grounds, some of which are pertinent to our discussion : The inheritance of wealth, culture, educational advantages, and economic opportunity tend toward the progressive increase of inequality, with an obvious effect upon character at both ends. Knowledge of exchange opportunities is not equally open to all. Too much foreknowledge is required and it is not available to all. In distribution, ethically, the whole process of valuation is a vicious circle, for price flows from demand, and demand from prices. Giving the public what it wants usually means corrupting the popular taste. The competitive system, as a want-creating and want-satisfying mechanism, falls far short of our highest ideals.

Yet, despite his onslaught, Professor Knight is not tempted to assert that possible alternatives to the system would be free from such defects. ' Radical critics of competition as a general basis of the economic order generally under-estimate egregiously the danger of doing vastly worse.'[2]

[1] *Ethics of Competition*, p. 79.   [2] Op. cit., p. 58.

When we are considering the ethical defects of the present system, with a view to judging whether curative medicine or drastic surgery is most appropriate, it will be found useful to distinguish carefully between the production and consumption of wealth. Much of the competition in production is necessary to secure fitness of means to ends, to cleanse and purify in a technical sense. Any rival system, however apostolic, would have to possess some substitutes for it, unless it were to become clogged and stagnant. Much of it is a reasonable consequence of personal liberty, and even of ethical responsibility. But competition on the side of consumption issues in emulations, rivalries, jealousies, social tyrannies, and false values and fashions of all kinds. It may be that these could be lifted and improved in ethical content, to the aim of really happier living, without touching the dynamic of production seriously. Fewer things might indeed be produced, but they could well be of more sustained value. Indeed, quality is never profitably sacrificed to quantity, and if the present age suffers from one affliction more than another, it is in the excess of impressions beyond its capacity to utilize and absorb them in permanent happiness. If a contrast is desired to illustrate the distinction I make, let us refer to the extraordinary difference between American development on the production and consumption side of economic activity respectively during the past twenty years. In production processes they have led the world in meticulous economy in the use of materials, of by-products, and in reclamations of all kinds ; they have developed a technique of scientific utilization of both material and labour, and in the elimination of waste nothing has seemed too insignificant for notice. It was well said that in the stockyards of Chicago everything of the pig was used except the squeal—probably by now even this is taken up for 'noises off' in the cinema. At the same time, in the consumption of wealth, the utmost lavishness, duplication, and waste prevailed, at any rate until the great depression, and little effort was exerted to make things last, to get the most out of carefully chosen possessions. It was a sign of success to lead the way in economy in production, and in lavish disregard of consequences in consumption.

' Waste is the greatest affront to the Christian consciousness, and especially waste of human effort.'[1] So the modern capitalist is ' Christian ' in his factory, and pagan in his private life—which is contrary to the common view !

THE ETHICS OF COMMUNISM

One of the most important discussions to-day rages round the claims of Communism to be more ethical, or even more Christian. We begin

[1] Lee, *Social Implications of Christianity*, p. 89.

with those who take the early Christian example as evidence that such a system was intended, in a state of purity of heart, to be a world type, for all ages.

The comments upon the apostolic experiment in Communism are legion. To Dr. Ryder Smith the failure was due to the ' error of precipitancy ' and a shortage in ' perfect meekness.' Stanley Jones says it failed because it was Communism of consumption only and not a Communism of production as well. ' No Christian Communism could succeed that did not take in both.' (The implication being that it would succeed if it *did* take in both.) It also failed because it was only part of the total order. It must be ' all or none.' But we know how Professor Bellerby gets over this ' island Communism ' difficulty. H. G. Wood says that, not only did it not touch production, but also it did not merge private households into communal centres. It was a brotherhood of the common table.[1]

' " Communism " has been distinguished from " Socialism " (whether democratic or not) on the basis of individuality, which it overrides or ignores, whereas Socialism, or, as we should now say, the Authoritarian State, is a reaction from the break-up of excessive individualism, and does not eliminate differences, but harmonizes them. Communist unity is like that of a

---

[1] *Communism—Christian and Marxist*, p. 23. This should be studied on the whole subject.

jelly-fish, different parts of which are hardly distinguishable from each other : the " Socialist " unity is like that of a human body, where the single life of the whole absolutely depends on the diversity of the parts alike in form and function.'[1]

Communism gets over the challenge of individuality by making promises of greater eventual scope for individual initiative, but whether it can ever give it and remain Communistic is doubtful. H. G. Wood holds, on the contrary, that the system logically must lead to the abolition of the family.[2]

Can we admit the claim that Communism is essentially more Christian, when we find that it is atheistic in fact, not by mere passive indifference to religion, but by active and vicious attack upon it ? And yet it is possible to see in it a purpose which to some is almost more religious than a profession of Christianity—that purpose is true equality in a universal brotherhood, and for this the individual is prepared to sink his own individuality. He would say that it is ' equality and freedom,' and here we should join issue as to the meaning of freedom, if his choice of vocation and location are alike formed for him in the general plan. The critic sees that, outside of profession, the Christian Churches do

[1] Archbishop William Temple on ' The Church,' in *Foundations*, p. 349.

[2] Op. cit., p. 18.

not, in fact, passionately support the establishment of a ' world of human society of free and equal brotherhood '[1]—rather they are on the defensive for the *status quo*. We may, I think, admit the danger, but submit the practical fact that Christianity is in the leadership for brotherhood, with a richer connotation than that of Communism, and that the conception of every man having an immortal soul for which Christ died, if we can vitally hold it, is a greater dynamic to free equality in social and economic affairs than any Communist ideals of the process of history, hatred of the old religion, tyrannies over the human mind, and depraved assertion of other equalities where they do not really exist.

H. G. Wells goes so far as to say that the Communist errs considerably in his exaggeration of the power and sincerity of the proletarian sentiment of brotherhood, and has developed this alleged disposition to fraternity with ' an inspiring but misleading cant.'[2]

Christianity and rationalism are seen to be completely repugnant to each other. For each nation tends to appropriate the Christian God into a tribal God, and warring natives appeal to the same God for victory and justification. The fundamental characteristic of religion has been said to be ' an expression of community,'

[1] MacMurray, op. cit., p. 25.
[2] *Work, Wealth, and Happiness of Mankind*, p. 304.

and Christianity, as a universal religion, must transcend the political organization and boundaries of our day. The critic says that in fact there is no community, and therefore Christianity has no reality as religion, and the Communist finds it a divider and not a solvent.

It has been rightly said that if religion protects against the fear of the unknown and of the future, the increasing dependence of man upon the community, his helplessness as a parasite upon his environment, should mean the development of a higher intensity of religion. But the Communist, considering religion as a need only of primitive society, and its promise of another and better life, with a special way thereto, as an anodyne for the ills of an unachieved economic harmony, finds that as he achieves an economic heaven on earth, so the need of compensations or dreams of future bliss recede—man has become an adult, independent of the religious props of the infancy of his evolution.

But the moment Christianity asserts the spiritual values of immortality and not its compensations for mortal values, and the moment it penetrates human consciousness with a sense of love which is eternal and divine, all the economic Utopias of Communism, and barren joys of equality and dubious freedom in a narrow range of time and space, seem to become feeble thrusts of the human spirit.

Mm

COMMUNISM AND EQUAL REWARD

It may fairly be said that, so far in the world's experience, experiments in Communistic principles of equal reward have not been large enough or permanent enough to give us any confident basis of judgement. My own view is that no really considerable output will be attainable by a complex industrial community, where the results of effort are exchanged by processes very distant and unrelated, whether for individual ' profit ' or for ' communal good,' without ' fear ' and ' self-interest ' as negative and positive incentives. And if this output is not attainable, high real wages are not attainable either, because total wages are limited by total production.

It must take many, many generations, in my judgement, 'to raise the standard of motivation, for the multitude of workers, to any common higher plane of service regardless of comparative personal reward. Yet the more businesses can use and press non-financial incentives of pride and self-respect, and make them common form, and the less completely the money-reward incentive dominates the field, the easier will it be to make large transfers to the higher motives of a new order. Clearly the immediate gains of this process must not obviously revert to the pockets of a few employers, or non-working ' shareholders '—it must benefit the community more directly, definitely, and impersonally.

The pulpit will gain nothing by urging systems which are based—or valid only—on a theory of non-financial incentives for the mass of workers in this age. Every careful student of possible systems, even those most disposed to an altered state of affairs, warns us against this mistake. Professor Bellerby's idealistic work, to which I am so indebted, is described by one of our ministerial colleagues as ' bold, even revolutionary in parts, but well balanced and essentially Christian '[1] : its fundamental conception is that character is the basis of the economic system. ' No change in the structure of the economic system should be attempted which goes *radically* beyond the powers of human character.' Professor MacGregor puts it : ' A theory of wages fails if it pretends to a view of labour in which an industry *could* not work.'

Professor Halm claims that an economy on Socialist or Communist lines forgoes the stimulus to good service which lies in the capitalistic connexion between economic calculation and income. ' Those who advocate economic planning are at this point in the position of having to count upon a change of the general attitude towards economic life, without being able to evince any presumption of its reliability or any

[1] The Rev. Percy Carden, *London Quarterly and Holborn Review*, January 1936, p. 99.

reason why it should come about at all.' Moreover, a decline in individual responsibility means
an inevitable expansion of the central auditing
apparatus.[1]

THE ETHICS OF SOCIAL CREDIT

We are looking, in this Lecture, only at those
questions of method which have come recently
to the fore in their claims to possess a special
ethical quality superior to that allowed or
evinced by the present method. After Communism, we may take Social Credit, and other
analogous schemes. An earnest correspondent
of mine, a member of the English Christian
Social Council, wrote to me recently that the
report of a conference on the Christian Approach
to Economic Reconstruction gave Monetary
Reform ' as a major task of the immediate
future.' But he was too wise to believe that this
could be solved by the light of Christian aspira-
tion or direction, and sought technical guidance.
His own notes on Monetary Reform involved the
abolition of bank interest, control of the issue of
new money, legislation for unemployment relief
pay, a price-level fixed on a standard-of-living
index, an excess profits tax, a surtax, and limited
dividend. I submit that Christian enthusiasm
for a better order may give an impetus to study

[1] In *Collectivist Economic Planning*, by various authors, 1935,
pp. 192, 200.

these problems, but no guidance whatever in their solution, and a rationalist might be just as eager for their solution, or as clear-headed in the process.

The religious qualities often alleged to be implicit in the Social Credit scheme, or the appeal to 'Christian principle,' no doubt have done something to commend it to pulpits and religious platforms. A rector of my acquaintance, who kept it out of his Sunday sermons, was an ardent advocate of it in his week-night lectures and guild meetings, tacitly assuming that in supporting it he was 'extending the Kingdom,' and painfully surprised when I questioned his wisdom. The impressive prestige of the Dean of Canterbury is perhaps of no little value in this direction, though the claims he makes are admittedly restrained in tone. In one pamphlet he is content to conclude, after declaring the gains of Socialist, Liberal, Conservative, and Democrat from Social Credit : 'The Christian gains from it—it gives to personality the true environment for growth and has regard for the worth of every single life.'[1] But in another, *Social Credit and the War on Poverty*,[2] he extols machinery as a 'child of Christendom '—' God's gift in response to man's quest. Let us beware how we mishandle it. There is a deeply significant way in which we may regard the genesis of machinery. At one

[1] *Why Poverty in the Midst of Plenty ?*, p. 24. [2] pp. 28–30.

end of a long process we may hear the words of Christ, uttered in respect of food and clothing : " Your heavenly Father knoweth that ye have need of all these things . . . seek ye first the Kingdom of God and His righteousness, and all these things shall be added unto you." In the middle of the process we see a social order, which we call Christendom, growing stable and co-operative, with schools and colleges arising and flourishing, scientists engaged in the pursuit of pure truth, and inventors in their quest. And finally at this, the far end of the process, we see machines pouring out such an abundance as makes want ridiculous and even criminal. It is the gift of God and the literal fulfilment of the pregnant words of Christ. Religious men have, therefore, of all others, substantial grounds for welcoming the machine, *and the National Discount and Dividend which unclamp its fetters*. They, beyond all others, regard with horror a money mechanism which to-day works havoc with machines, smothers inventions at birth, drives producers against their natural desires to curtail output and workers to ca' canny, which flings God's gift, as it were, back in His face.'

Father H. Drinkwater, in *Why not End Poverty?*, declares: 'Cheap money! The very words are an insult to God and His commandments ! Money is not a commodity to be bought or sold.'[1]

[1] Op. cit., 1935, p. 8.

He restates the Catholic position on usury over
the centuries with a curious hankering after the
current validity of medieval ideas, and brings
in the Credit schemes with practical effect for
the support of Catholic schools : ' Even if
religious prejudice prevented credits being issued
directly for Catholic school buildings, still all
Catholic citizens would have their full share of
the general-consumer credit issues, or national
dividend, and would be able to subscribe to
their own school-building funds just as they do
now, but far more liberally. . . . Every Catholic
who cares for Catholic schools . . . who believes
there is such a thing as social justice at all,
should rise to the occasion, and put every ounce
of effort into the urgent task of restoring to this
nation the power over its own money.'[1] The
poverty he proposes to abolish is that of
Matt. xxv. 31–46, and not that of the technical
Catholic sense—the life of the Holy Family or
the poverty of monks and nuns. ' The earth is
the Lord's and the fullness thereof, and He has
given it to us, His family of children, for all to
share : *that* is the solid reason for the National
Dividend.'[2]

The Rev. John Knowles, in *Social Credit and
Christian Ideals*, devotes a small book to the
identification indicated in his title. ' Since our
examination is confined to the moral and
religious effects of Social Credit we cannot turn

[1] Op. cit., pp. 45–6.   [2] Op. cit., p. 69.

aside to examine the soundness of the Douglas scheme. This can best be done by a careful study of the writings of Major Douglas and others.' He admits that ' we must not hastily equate the material abundance which Social Credit provides with the abundant life which Christ purposes for men ' (John x. 10). He declares that the problem which the Christian Church must solve is ' how to make the Money Power our servant, not our master. A way to solve this problem has been made known in the writings and speeches of Major Douglas.' The financial system makes Christian practice well-nigh impossible. ' We feel sure the Directors of the Bank of England do not realize that, while the Gadarene System besought Christ to depart, the Banking System compels Christ to go, not only from " dark Satanic mills," but also from " England's pleasant pastures." ' ' If the present financial conventions cannot be changed, Christianity is doomed . . . we would like to turn from this Frankenstein of finance to consider the sane and natural use of what is perhaps man's greatest invention, money. Space forbids. To condense would only be to obscure. We must refer interested readers to the Social Credit literature, and ask them to think out the implications.'[1]

In Australia, Social Credit seems to have made no little headway as a religious question. The *Monthly Miracle* claims to be the ' Trumpeter of

[1] Op. cit., pp. 18, 67.

the Credit Crusade,' and is full of scriptural injunction and reference. In an explanatory catechism on the ' Wice Currency,' Question 17 asks, ' Should the Church touch politics or economics ? '—and the answer is, ' The Church should touch politics and economics to the extent of enunciating the life-giving principle of natural law, as that part of God's will that has been revealed. In order to get *men* right it is necessary to give men right. The Church is responsible for the interpretation it places upon revealed law. It cannot shirk the responsibility if it accept the charge of preaching the gospel to every creature. The gospel is truth. Truth prevails in the political and economic spheres. The Church has a duty to seek and to preach economic law.'[1] What this law is, the context does not fail to assure us. Another issue says, ' The platform, the pulpit, the pew, and the forum must unite in demanding legal sanctions for a credit economy, so that you may live in love and charity with your neighbour. It is not enough to preach the love of God. By legislation you must by intention issue a money with which you can practise the love of thy neighbour.'[2] Again, ' The brotherhood of man comes in peace, not in fratricidal conflicts with those who differ from us. To get righteous money we must give up the unrighteous mammon.'[3]

[1] *Monthly Miracle*, January 10, 1936.
[2] Ibid., February 10, 1934.
[3] Ibid., January 10, 1936.

' " Seek first the Kingdom of God and His righteousness," in the economic realm, is to be interpreted in a monetary system intended to accord with economic law by which man replenishes and subdues the earth.'[1] ' Bringing money into accord with truth will show the unfolding of the complete plan for the working of the laws of God. New money opens up the long road that all must travel in living for the work of the Lord.'[2] ' Crusader ' breaks into poetry on ' The Celestial Plan,' which concludes :

For the mind of man is widening with the process of the suns;
The plan that's now unfolding leads where celestial purpose runs.

On the new currency, ' Freewice,' in ' The Auguries of Freedom ' (after—a long way after !—William Blake), says :

The want expressed ! The human need :
To meet demand, supply be freed.

.   .   .   .

When men give heed to think it out,
Credit will free the world from debt.
The wise will read the Will of God
In every blessing from the sod.

.   .   .   .

Would you hear the inspired Word ?
Use honest money for the Lord.[3]

[1] *Monthly Miracle*, October 10, 1935.
[2] Ibid., March 12, 1935.
[3] Ibid., July 10, 1935.

In a report on monetary reform in New Zealand—where Douglas schemes have been making a great stir—the journal quotes from the *Elector*, Christchurch, November 1935 : ' Auckland clergy of all denominations joined in a public resolution—" Continuance of civic and political ineptitude, on the part of this or any other Government, is warranted, not only to destroy faith in constitutional government, but also to do despite to the essential spirit of Christianity." Prosperity and progress—" The first step to that goal is monetary reform." '[1] It is no doubt all very crude and callow, but that does not indicate that it is not very effective.

A very earnest correspondent of my own recently begged me to back him in preparing a pamphlet for industrialists, with a front page as follows :

RELIGION AND REALITY

CHRIST'S PRINCIPLES CAN NOW BE PUT INTO PRACTICE

TREAT THY NEIGHBOUR AS THYSELF

<u>YOU</u> CAN DO THIS BY EACH HAVING

MONEY

CAPITALIZE BRITAIN AND LET EACH FAMILY DRAW A YEARLY

NO WORK	DIVIDEND	NO DIVIDEND

[1] *Monthly Miracle*, December 10, 1935.

THE INVENTIONS OF YOUR ANCESTORS HAVE MADE THIS POSSIBLE. M A N IS SENT INTO THE WORLD TO REAP THAT WHEREON HE HAS BESTOWED NO LABOUR.

John iv. 38

THE RESPONSIBILITY RESTS ON

GOD IS IN		ARE IN GOD
HEAVEN	Y O U	ARE THE LIGHT
IS IN		OF THE WORLD

LEARN ABOUT THIS AND INSIST ON HAVING

S O C I A L   C R E D I T

AND LET EACH FAMILY DRAW £300 A YEAR

Part of the pamphlet ran :

'The man who formulated the principles I have enumerated before [Jesus Christ] also said, with that clarity of vision which is so distinguished a character of his utterances, that man is sent into the world to reap that thereon he has bestowed no labour. And this is quite true. The inventive genius of God working in man (i.e. co-operative leaning and effort) has so eased his burden of labour that, by artificial means, man reaps a hundredfold. But, far from benefiting by this bounteous crop, it is denied him by the unscrupulous and privileged position of a small minority. A system of social credit has been brilliantly devised whereby man, reaping the harvest sown by his inventive ancestors, could enjoy a yearly income on the basis of no work no income. This income, like the sun and rain, falls on the righteous and the unrighteous, the rich and poor, the strong and weak, and so can safely be commended *if* one accepts one of the foregoing principles—namely, treat thy neighbour as thyself. Now, gentlemen, I ask you to ally the principles for which Christ lived and died to a political movement. Let us be able to say a vote for us means a vote for God, common unity in well-being, a vote for us means a step nearer the Kingdom of Heaven—that is, the full realization of the desires and activities of the mind and body. We hereby adopt a policy of co-operation or common well-being based on the principle of treating our neighbour as ourselves. We propose to do this by introducing a yearly dividend, payable in moneys the issue of which is based on consumption, which in turn is based on production. We do not ask you to vote for a god of the dead, a king, or a country, but the living God in *us*, the Kingdom of Heaven in *us*. Let our slogans be : " Treat thy neighbour as thyself, and serve God six days a week and rest the seventh." If you adopt this policy, a policy which I am convinced will find a response in the heart and mind of every man and woman of sense and feeling, you can take Christ down from the cross where He has hung for 2,000 years and make Him your Prime Minister, the Kingdom of Heaven your country, and your common purpose that understanding and common relationship in the living man your God. It is then that your enemies will have to declare that they are the Anti-Christ, but against the just anger and hope of common well-being of the millions of the common living God their opposition will be as ineffectual as the snow before the sun, the dust before the storm. I tell you, if you will but go to the people with these principles and this policy set clearly before them, nothing can stand before you, and then may it later be possible for you to say the lion has lain down with the lamb, our swords may be beaten into ploughshares, there is no need any more for war among men. There is no longer any need to disguise the fact that the Second Coming, so eagerly awaited and so long delayed, has come, not as a person, doing wondrous deeds and clothed in shining raiment, but as a collection of ideas, clothed in coherence.'

At the moment of writing, I see a minister writing to his local paper in these terms :

' It is because Social Credit offers the fullest antidote to war, and on the other hand furnishes the most satisfactory instrument of social justice, that as a minister of the word of Christ I cannot but enter my protest against your correspondent's light dismissal of the subject.'[1]

These citations are only a few specimens of a considerable literature given to show that the Douglas Credit Scheme, with its outcome the National Dividend, has been claimed by many of its adherents to be the essential method of a more Christian order. There is no doubt that if the scheme were not a dangerous delusion it would be worthy of much that is claimed of it from the point of view of Christian principle. It is the best modern example of a *machinery* in which there is nothing essentially moral, but for which great ethical claims could be made if it would work. It perplexes so many men, especially those who are ' wishful ' thinkers, that I feel constrained to explain why I consider it as unworkable as a machine for perpetual motion, and therefore why the pulpit should have no lot or part in it, until the main body of reputable economic thinkers have declared it

[1] Extract from letter to the *West Cumberland Times*, May 2, 1936.

to be feasible. When that is demonstrated beyond doubt, the time may be ripe for its adoption with religious fervour. But as it is an interruption to my theme and an example only, I relegate this analysis to an Appendix.

CHAPTER V

CONCLUSION

MAY my final word be addressed directly to those for whom this book is mainly written? I have tried to make the point that a better machine presupposes a better man, and that the moral betterment of man individually is the peculiar province, opportunity, and responsibility of the preacher and teacher.[1] This betterment consists of three stages, in this order: conversion of the will; education of the moral sense; and last, when these make it feasible, an environment which gives the higher motive a chance to breathe, live, and succeed.

No brilliance in denunciation of social evils, the system, or the wickedness of those in control can atone for weakness or apathy or lack of skill in the arrest of the soul and spirit of the man in the pew.

There are some addresses and sermons that must give the average hearer a sense of satisfaction, not a sense of sin. He is presented with a complete moral alibi, a grievance against

[1] See especially 'The Social Function of the Church,' *Copec Commission Report*, vol. xi.

Providence, and the ' other fellow ' or society as a whole is always to blame. He is given little notion of his personal responsibility, but, instead, a hectic sense of his social rights.

But even if his ego is captured, the preacher's work is only just begun, and we have not risen so superior to the Decalogue that we can afford to extend its recital from a weekly to an annual exercise.

Every experienced minister knows that susceptibility to religious feeling and influence is not identical with moral or ethical sensibility. There is frequently, but by no means always, a close correlation between them, and even a rough, simple character, on conversion, often becomes one of sterling moral integrity. But quite frequently, and especially with emotional, unstable, or primitive types, education into a good moral standard is a slow and painful process. ' Conversion ' is an essential preliminary with such, but it is only a beginning. Nor need we postulate the presence of hypocrisy or cant. The religious fervour and experience may be very genuine, but it does not follow that there will be an acute sense of duty, of fidelity, of unselfishness, or any large degree of that superior ethical incentive which we are postulating as essential for a higher social order.

I use the term ' conversion ' to cover the wide range of religious psychological experiences, from a very vocal ' conviction of sin,' through repulsion at the old life, ' change of heart,' decision, to silent dedication. Canon Sheppard is surely right when he says Christianity stands or falls by its claim to give ordinary men ' power to become.' If we accept the fact that with the average person there is little likelihood of a superstructure of voluntary acceptance of the personal self-abnegations of the Christian ethic being attainable by the light of nature, this experience, in one or other of its forms, is an essential preliminary to any active motivation of the average person who makes up the mass, for such a higher order of society as we have been contemplating. It seems a formidable task to ' convert ' the whole of our population. But statistically it is easy enough. Assuming (*a*) that we ignore now the older people, but prepare for the future, (*b*) that the most suitable age is from fifteen to twenty, (*c*) that the numbers reaching that age could all be made to pass through our Church services of different denominations in this country—a big assumption in practice—then, if there were one ' conversion ' in every six services, the whole adult population would have passed through this experience in a generation. Of course, this would allow for a much lighter task in small communities, if the great missions could play their part on an appropriate scale. Viewed in this way, the complete evangelization of the community seems by no means insuperable.

But this experience is an ' acquired characteristic,' and as such is not specifically or traceably inheritable. In fact, the essence of the experience is that it must be personal. And this means that the effort of the preacher and evangelist is continuous, perpetual. Each age has its own Garden of Eden.

Whether, on biological principles, *susceptibility* to the psychological change would grow more or less, I am not prepared to hazard a guess.

But I have indicated that ' conversion,' like patriotism, is not enough, and that the educative process must follow, both by direct reiterated precept and by raising the common rule or expectation of social life. Now, this environment, unlike conversion, we may more justifiably expect would not be a question of *starting* afresh with each generation. It would be accumulative and accretional, and, when several successive generations had lived up to a higher Christian standard of altruism and self-sacrifice, it would create a new atmosphere, a new minimum of social conduct. If current motive usable in economic life is only the generalization of the ' done thing,' and even Christian living merely the best and freshest exposition of it, then the ' done thing ' would continually advance in ethical quality and practical width.

The Intellectual and the Spiritual Tasks of the Preacher

The educative process must not, of course, be merely negative, like the Decalogue, but aim at certain special objectives : first, in the realm of intellect, better thinking, cleansed from wishful delusion by the scientific method; second, in the realm of spirit, objects for life more calculated to attain a Christian welfare.

In the first of these, it will have been seen how much stress I place upon the peril or fallacy of generalization and composition. A thing that is excellent, standing relatively by itself in a world that is different, may be neither good nor sensible nor possible when it is made universal. If it derives its character from its difference, it makes nonsense when it is the same. The absolutes stand the change, the relatives do not. But every thought should be made to face the test before we dogmatize, and until we have worked it out we cannot tell absolutes from relatives. There is, too, the important fact that progress in certain directions is incompatible with progress in others. If, for instance, our ideal is to make man a perfect member of society, then we cannot, for certain, also make him a perfect individual. ' Most modern communities, particularly those of Russia and the United States, tend to produce a standardized man, relatively lacking in individuality, but able, for that very reason, to be a more efficient member of society.'[1]

This insistence springs, I suppose, from a feeling that, whatever may be the state of one's opinions and their coherence, public utterance of them should have a certain responsible quality, especially when one is taking advantage of a man in his hour of trust and faith, his critical faculties suspended, mind quiescent, and the wishful soul all alive, no desire or power to challenge. I feel it is taking a mean advantage of the occasion to push, through his emotions, our half-worked and unsynthesized thinking ; it is like giving him amateur advice about his car or his duodenum. So I plead for your rationalized preaching, with as little colour and impulse as may be—in just one corner of your work. For I cannot believe that starting false ideas, giving wrong twists, creating prejudices, gains advance in the long run. (In all this, I often have a haunting feeling that I am on the wrong tack ; that, for the mass of mankind, preaching must be non-mental, impulsive, picturesque, irrational, inaccurate, torrential, to do its work, and that by purifying and rationalizing it we rob it of its saving virtue. The defects of it are to be the inevitable price we pay for its achievement. The torrent or nothing. And yet surely the capture of the man's own moral citadel should be sufficient scope for those

[1] J. W. N. Sullivan, *Contemporary Mind.*

particular attributes of great preaching which
are not cold facts and bare syllogism, and I may
be allowed my plea for unemotional appeal in
the realm of method.)

Coming, then, to these second aims—the ends
of life—the most prominent is service or self-
sacrifice, a fear of parasitism and uselessness
in place of a popular deadly ' equivalence.' I
do not agree with all Bernard Shaw's applications of the Sermon on the Mount, but he was
quite of my mind when he said a gentleman
was one who tries to put into society at least as
much as he takes out of it. Dr. Lindsay calls
' the most sinister of our social divisions the
disastrous division of men into those who do
good to other people and those who only have
good done to them.'[1] Einstein has said, ' A
hundred times every day I remind myself that
my inner and outer life depend on the labours of
other men, living and dead, and that I must
exert myself in order to give in the same measure
as I have received and am still receiving. I am
strongly drawn to the simple life, and am often
oppressed by the feeling that I am engrossing an
unnecessary amount of the labour of my fellow
men.'[2]

In one of Mr. H. G. Wells's pregnant utterances, self-surrender is the supreme test : ' Is it
any wonder that to this day the Galilean is too
much for our small hearts ? '

[1] *Christianity and Economics*, p. 144.   [2] *The World as I See It.*

The Archbishop of York said recently with great justice that ' Christianity lays upon personality a stress unknown in any other religion or philosophy, except so far as these have learnt from the gospel. Its doctrine of the true relation of men to one another is not that they are jostling atoms where each respects the rights of others only because that is the way to win respect for his own ; it is rather that we belong to one another in the fellowship of the community, and each can be truly himself only in the interdependence of that fellowship.' Mere self-surrender or self-sacrifice is not in all cases the highest Christian motive. ' We have no evidence that the consummation of self-surrender would be more morally effectual than the consummation of self-interests.'[1] It boggles the economic imagination to picture the actual working of a productive society in which *literally* every one insists in sacrificing himself all the time to every one else. Nothing would hold the traffic up worse than insisting on ' after you, please ' at every inconvenient bottle-neck on the highway. The sense of interdependence and solidarity of society includes that kind of service which is self-insistent as well as self-effacing. The greatest may be truly the servant of all, but he is nevertheless the greatest. Precedence is the key to order, which is heaven's first law. For the last to submit to being first may be the greatest

[1] Lee, op. cit., p. 56.

surrender, after all.[1] It may be said that this sense of service is not the monopoly of Christianity, and can indeed exist without it.[2] True, but in the average man the sense of service can exist much better and more easily with the Christian ideal. For we can hardly exaggerate the extent to which it is vital to the New Testament in a sense in which it is not to any other ethical system.

Again, treating the content of Christianity as everything that the non-Christian ethic does not possess independently without it, we should absorb all developing truth into its impetus and implication. For thereby we put every new item of knowledge on to the power-house, and bring it to the service of the common man with a Christian dynamic. We do nothing more than Erasmus urged : ' Everything which the peoples and religions have invested with ethical values he desired to see adopted into Christianity as an element of fruitfulness ; and, though living in an epoch of narrow-minded and dogmatic fanaticism, this great humanist was able to deliver the splendid dictum : " Wherever you encounter truth, look upon it as Christianity." Therewith a bridge was built, linking up all times and all zones.'[3]

[1] I think instinctively of the self-effacing Dr. Salazar, called from the university chair which he loved, to be Prime Minister of Portugal.
[2] Plato had a very developed sense of the interdependence of the parts of society, and its corollary of social service, which became a minute regulator of personal behaviour.
[3] Stefan Zweig, *Erasmus.*

THE USE OF UTOPIAS

I hope that nothing that I have said will lead you to think I underrate the stimulus of Utopias and impracticable ideals. The construction of Utopias has great personal value, for it makes us dig deep into the roots of motive and ponder the ends of life. But too commonly we do not trace out what is objectively possible to a given state of character; we adopt the objective society and assume the necessary character. As Professor Whitehead says : ' The ideals cherished in the souls of men enter into the character of their actions. These interactions within society modify the social laws by modifying the occasions to which those laws apply. Impracticable ideals are a programme for reform. Such a programme is not to be criticized by immediate possibilities. Progress consists in modifying the laws of nature so that the Republic on Earth may conform to that society to be discerned ideally by the divination of wisdom.'[1] But the mere reading of such delightful ideal commonwealths as Bacon's *New Atlantis*, More's *Utopia*, Campanella's *City of the Sun*, Plutarch's *Lycurgus*, or the creative fancies of H. G. Wells, has no greater intellectual value or moral quality than we put into it. Bosanquet protests that to throw our ideas into the future is the death of all idealism. Too great a preoccupation with

[1] A. N. Whitehead, *Adventures of Ideas*.

distant objectives may hinder practical progress. The stars give us absolute direction, but
by reliance on them all the time we may walk
into the river. The Scotch parson's specific,
' Look up for guidance, down for safety,' may
be prescribed for social idealism too.

' Otherworldliness ' is not a virtue if your
object is social and goes beyond personal holi-
ness. You are rendering no service towards a
better order if you overstress as *a social criterion*
certain ethical principles which have only a
personal or a limited application. By too great an
insistence upon one particular good principle—
where all good principles have a right to live,
and the surrender of one principle to another is
equal in ethical value to the surrender of one self-
interest to another—you may throttle the good
results of any of them. And a religious idea,
above all, carried to monopolistic excess, can
create a tyranny like none other. ' Thus, in the
case of the Hindus, the desire for knowledge of
the human body and its functions gave way
before a religious idea. We have only to imagine
a widespread growth of the teachings of Christian
Science, and the gradual disappearance of
Western medical knowledge can easily be
conceived.'[1]

Many Christian saints have qualified their
spirituality with too much self-consciousness.
' A successful apostle must have rather a worldly

[1] Alderton Pink, *A Realist Looks on Democracy*.

mind, because he needs to have his hand on the pulse of the world.'[1]

SPECIALISTS IN ECONOMIC REFORM

I am only in line with Dr. Lindsay and other students when I conclude that the real task of the pulpit is not primarily with the technique of the political and economic machine at all, although I would welcome occasional instances of men with a real aptitude for it undergoing the necessary discipline and study, fully equal in time and attention to that which they would have to give to any other expert or professional curriculum. The real task is the conversion and elevation of the human motive, on such a scale that new organism may become possible ; inspiration for the tasks of life as well as the destinies of death. Men ought to get from their religion a ' sense of how high and worthy a vocation politics and social administration may be. To urge men to do such work, to give their very best to it, is the Church's business—to tell them how to do it is not.'[2]

Dr. Temple says the pulpit may feel bound to leave it to experts to diagnose the disease and prescribe the remedy ; but that it is the Christian duty to incite the experts, even if need be to badger the experts, until they produce their answer to the problem. By all means goad

[1] Santayana, *Platonism and the Spiritual Life*, p. 39.
[2] Lindsay, op. cit., p. 139.

and badger the expert, and even—as my own experience indicates—get easy applause from your own responsive congregations by mildly taunting him for the world's mess. Prevent him from becoming the complacent custodian of economic inevitability. When the economic expert shows signs of relapsing into a museum attendant, incite him to new activity. Be his amplifier for the groans of humanity.

But, in all this, remember that it is just conceivable he is not so cold-blooded or apathetic as may appear ; he may be as deeply concerned as you, and that anxiety may be a secret spring of his calm toil. He may be patiently analysing, testing, and winning his inches of the way forward while you are spending your time wringing your hands and alternately scolding and giving directions.

On ' Experts '

Moreover, this expertise business cuts both ways. If you have agreed with me that a better order is compounded of character and machinery, of motive and method, then you are looking at him as an expert in method, and he is equally entitled to look at you as an expert in motive, to ask whether you are ' delivering the goods,' whether you are *really* in the great line of power over the character and souls of men. He may say that he will be ready with the better machine when you produce the better motive that it demands and presupposes. He may plead that it has not been his business to study the best way into the spirit of man, to convert man with the hidden spiritual force, to ' cure souls,' or even to educate motive to the highest end. For that demands expert study of developing human psychology, a special call, gifts of speech and personality, and a technique which is both a spiritual art and science. He may suggest that, under the great truth ' Jesus Christ, the same yesterday, to-day, and for ever,' you are smugly resting, without moving closely with the minds of men which develop so rapidly under the pressures of modernity. It may even be the economist's job to ' badger ' the parson into producing better men with which to remake society. The truth is, the minister and the economist are the two sides of the same coin, but that is a bad analogy, for they ought to be constantly looking at each other.

But I see no reason why the Church should not develop its own experts, adding to their main calling an attainment in other fields which commands the respect of the professional exponents. It should encourage a few of its number to be highly skilled in apologetics, as in exegetical studies ; in psychology, law, biology, and eugenics ; in the natural sciences ; in public administration and local government ; and, last but not least, a few to suffer the full rigours of economic analysis and statistical technique. To write or speak vaguely, warmly, and categorically on social reform is not enough ; social reform must come last in the economic curriculum. After full mastery of the theory of value, the nature of price and rent, and all the horrid jargon of currency, margins, indifference curves, and coefficients of correlation, shall the student win his right to the lush pastures of emotion, indignation, and pontification. Frankly, short courses of lectures on social problems, and readings in the atmosphere of economics without tears, while excellent for general purposes, do not satisfy this requirement. They may be good in themselves, but they are the peptonized food of ready-made conclusions, and tempt the student to think he has ' done ' the subject. To do any good with it in the mind, you must get a headache ; to do any good with it in the world, a heartache.

Such specialists—and we have already recognized the principle in certain directions—might be a great source of strength to the Christian Church, bonding its fabric into the structure of society at many critical points ; and they need be no worse evangelists and pastors for all that.

．　．　．　．　．　．　．　．

H. G. Wells joins the prophets when he says, ' The desire for service, for subordination . . . is the undying element in every religious system.

. . . The first sentence in the modern creed must be, not " I believe," but " I give myself." To what ? and how ? are the questions to which we must address ourselves.'[1] But to answer them is surely to say again, ' I believe.' We remake our own creed, and all the new knowledge goes into it, and still it will be too empty for the fullness of life.

.   .   .   .

If we trod the deeps of ocean, if we struck the stars in rising,
If we wrapped the globe intensely with one hot electric breath,
'Twere but power within our tether, no new spirit power comprising,
And in life we were not greater men, nor bolder men in death.[2]

[1] *The Open Conspiracy*, p. 25.
[2] Elizabeth Barrett Browning, ' Lady Geraldine's Courtship,' 1844.

APPENDIX I

THE ECONOMIC CANON OF THE
NEW TESTAMENT

I. The Four Gospels

Possessions (*General*)

Mark x.	21	*The Ruler with Great Possessions.* 'Go, sell all thou hast, and distribute [give] unto the poor.'
Matt. xix.	21	
Luke xviii.	22	

'How hardly shall they that have riches enter into the kingdom of heaven. . . . It is easier for a camel to go through a needle's eye than for a rich man to enter into the kingdom of God.'

Matt. xxvii.	57	*Joseph of Arimathaea,* 'a rich man' . . . 'a counsellor of honourable estate' . . . 'who also himself was Jesus' disciple' . . . 'a good man and a righteous.'
Mark xv.	43	
Luke xxiii.	51	

Matt. v.	40	'And if any man would go to law with thee, and take away thy coat, let him have thy cloke also.'
Luke vi.	29	

Luke iii.	11	'He that hath two coats, let him impart to him that hath none; and he that hath food, let him do likewise.'

Matt. xiii.	12	'For whosoever hath, to him shall be given, and he shall have abundance: but whosoever hath not, from him shall be taken away even that which he hath.'
xxv.	29	
Mark iv.	25	
Luke viii.	18	
xix.	26	

Matt. xiii.   31 ⎫ *The Grain of Mustard Seed,* ' which
Luke xiii.   19 ⎭ a man took, and sowed in his field '
                 . . . ' and cast into his own garden.'

Matt. vi.   19 ⎫ ' Lay not up for yourselves treasures
Luke xii.   33 ⎭ upon the earth, where moth and rust
                 doth consume, and where thieves
                 break through and steal ;
                 ' But lay up for yourselves treasures
                 in heaven. . . .'
                 ' Sell that ye have, and give
                 alms. . . .'

Matt. vi.   24 ⎫ ' Ye cannot serve God and mam-
Luke xvi.   13 ⎭ mon.'

Matt. vi.   25 ⎫ ' Be not anxious for your life, what
Luke xii.   22 ⎪ ye shall eat, or what ye shall drink ;
Matt. vi.   31 ⎪ nor yet for your body, what ye shall
Luke xii.   29 ⎭ put on.'
                 ' For all these things do the nations
                 of the world seek after. . . .'
                 ' Seek ye first his kingdom . . . and
                 these things shall be added unto
                 you.'

Matt. vii.   11 ⎫ ' If ye . . . know how to give good
Luke xi.   13 ⎭ gifts unto your children, how much
                 more shall your Father which is in
                 heaven give [good things] [the Holy
                 Spirit] to them that ask him ? '

Matt. xviii. 12 ⎫ ' If any man have a hundred sheep,
Luke xv.   4 ⎭ and one of them be gone astray,
                 doth he not leave the ninety and
                 nine [in the wilderness], and seek
                 that which goeth astray . . . ? '

Matt. xx.   *Parable of the Labourers in the Vine-*
                 yard (*vide* p. 207).

Matt. xxi.   *Parable of the Two Sons and the*
                 Father's Vineyard.

Luke xii.   *Parable of the Rich Fool.* ' Soul, thou hast much goods laid up for many years ; take thine ease, eat, drink, be merry. . . .'

Luke xix. 2 ' And, behold, there was a man named Zacchaeus, which was the chief among the publicans, and he was rich.'

    8-10 ' And Zacchaeus stood, and said unto the Lord : Behold, Lord, the half of my goods I give to the poor ; and if I have taken any thing from any man by false accusation, I restore him fourfold.

      ' And Jesus said unto him, This day is salvation come to this house, for so much as he also is a son of Abraham.

      ' For the Son of man is come to seek and to save that which was lost.'

POSSESSIONS (*Specific*)

Luke xv. 8-10 ' Either what woman having ten pieces of silver, if she lose one piece, doth not light a candle, and sweep the house, and seek diligently till she find it :

      ' And when she hath found it, she calleth her friends and her neighbours together, saying, Rejoice with me; for I have found the piece which I had lost.

      ' Likewise, I say unto you, there is joy in the presence of the angels of God over one sinner that repenteth.'

Mark iii.   27 ⎤
Matt. xii.   29 ⎬   ' No one can enter into the house of
Luke xi.   21-2 ⎦   the strong man, and spoil his goods,
except he first bind the strong man,
and then he will spoil his house.'

RICH AND POOR

Mark xiv.   3 ⎤   *The Alabaster Box of Ointment.*
Matt. xxvi.   6 ⎬   ' For this ointment might have been
(Luke vii.   36) ⎦   sold for above three hundred pence
and *given to the poor. . . .*'
' For ye have the poor always with
you, and whensoever ye will ye can
do them good.'

John xii.   3   *The Costly Pound of Ointment of
Spikenard.*
Judas : ' Why was not this ointment
sold for three hundred pence, and
given to the poor ? . . . (Not that he
cared for the poor. . . .) '
Jesus : ' For the poor ye have always
with you, but me ye have not
always.'

Luke vi.   20 ⎤   ' Blessed are ye poor : for yours is
         21*a* ⎦   the kingdom of God.'
[Matt. v. 3 adds, ' in spirit.']
' Blessed are ye that hunger now :
for ye shall be filled.'
[Matt. v. 6 adds, ' and thirst after
righteousness.']

Luke xvi. 19-31   ' There was a certain rich man, which
was clothed in purple and fine linen,
and fared sumptuously every day :
' And there was a certain beggar
named Lazarus, which was laid at his
gate, full of sores,

Luke xvi. 19-31
(continued)

' And desiring to be fed with the crumbs which fell from the rich man's table : moreover the dogs came and licked his sores.

' And it came to pass, that the beggar died, and was carried by the angels into Abraham's bosom : the rich man also died and was buried ;

' And in hell he lifted up his eyes, being in torments, and seeth Abraham afar off, and Lazarus in his bosom.

' And he cried and said, Father Abraham, have mercy on me, and send Lazarus, that he may dip the tip of his finger in water, and cool my tongue ; for I am tormented in this flame.

' But Abraham said, Son, remember that thou in thy lifetime receivedst thy good things, and likewise Lazarus evil things ; but now he is comforted and thou art tormented.

' And beside all this, between us and you there is a great gulf fixed : so that they which would pass from hence to you cannot ; neither can they pass to us, that would come from thence.

' Then he said, I pray thee therefore, father, that thou wouldest send him to my father's house :

' For I have five brethren ; that he may testify unto them, lest they also come into this place of torment.

' Abraham saith unto him, They have Moses and the prophets ; let them hear them.

Luke xvi. 19-31 *(continued)*		' And he said, Nay, father Abraham : but if one went unto them from the dead, they will repent. ' And he said unto him, If they hear not Moses and the prophets, neither will they be persuaded, though one rose from the dead.'
Matt. xi. Luke vii.	5 } 22 }	' And the poor have good tidings preached to them.'

INCIDENTAL REFERENCES TO RICHES AND POVERTY

Mark iv. Matt. xiii. Luke viii.	19 } 22 } 14 }	*The Parable of the Sower.* ' The deceitfulness of riches . . . choke the word and it becometh unfruitful.' ' [Riches] bring no fruit to perfection.'
Mark viii. Matt. xvi. Luke ix.	36 } 26 } 25 }	' For what shall it profit a man, to gain the whole world and forfeit his life ? '
Mark xii. Luke xxi.	44 } 1 }	' Rich men were casting their gifts into the treasury . . . a poor widow cast in two mites . . . this poor widow cast in more than they all, for they all do cast in of their superfluity, but she of her want did cast in all the living that she had.'

LANDLORD AND TENANTS

Mark xii. 1-11 Matt. xxi. 33-41 Luke xx. 9-16	} } }	*The Parable of the Vineyard.* ' There was a man that was a householder, which planted a vineyard, and set a hedge about it, and digged a winepress in it and built a tower, and *let it out* to husbandmen.'

Mark xii. 1-11 ⎫
Matt.xxi. 33-41 ⎬
Luke xx. 9-16 ⎭
(continued)

He was an absentee . . . went into another country 'for a long time.' He sent servants to collect 'his fruits' and they were killed. Jesus asked what he would do to the husbandmen, and the reply was, 'He will miserably destroy those miserable men, and will let out the vineyard unto other husbandmen, which shall render him the fruits in their seasons' (Matt.).

[Two Gospels say merely, ' give the vineyard to others.']

CONTRACT AND SERVICE

Matt. xx. 1-16

' For the kingdom of heaven is like unto a man that is an householder, which went out early in the morning to hire labourers into his vineyard.

' And when he had agreed with the labourers for a penny a day, he sent them into his vineyard.

' And he went out about the third hour, and saw others standing idle in the market-place.

' And said unto them : Go ye also into the vineyard, and whatsoever is right I will give you. And they went their way.

' Again he went out about the sixth and ninth hour, and did likewise.

' And about the eleventh hour he went out, and found others standing idle, and saith unto them, Why stand ye here all the day idle ?

Matt. xx. 1-16
(*continued*)

' They say unto him, Because no man hath hired us. He saith unto them, Go ye also into the vineyard ; and whatsoever is right, that shall ye receive.

' So when even was come, the lord of the vineyard saith unto his steward, Call the labourers, and give them their hire, beginning from the last unto the first.

' And when they came that were hired about the eleventh hour, they received every man a penny.

' But when the first came, they supposed that they should have received more ; and they likewise received every man a penny.

' And when they had received it, they murmured against the goodman of the house,

' Saying, These last have wrought but one hour, and thou hast made them equal unto us, which have borne the burden and heat of the day.

' But he answered one of them, and said, Friend, I do thee no wrong : didst not thou agree with me for a penny ?

' Take that thine is, and go thy way : I will give unto this last, even as unto thee.

' Is it not lawful for me to do what I will with mine own ? Is thine eye evil, because I am good ?

' So the last shall be first, and the first last : for many be called, but few chosen.'

Matt. v.	41	' And whosoever shall compel thee to go one mile, go with him twain.'
Matt. vii. Luke vi.	12 }	' All things, therefore, whatsoever ye would that men should do unto you, even so do ye also unto them [likewise].'
Matt.xviii.23-35		A certain king made a reckoning with his servants. . . . One had not wherewith to pay and his lord commanded him to be sold, and his wife, and children, and all that he had, and payment to be made. . . . The lord, being moved with compassion, released him and forgave him the debt. That servant found one of his fellow servants which owed him a hundred pence . . . and cast him into prison, till he should pay that which was due.

SERVANTS

Matt. xxiv.	46 }	*The Faithful and Wise Servant [Steward].* ' Blessed is that servant, whom his lord when he cometh shall find so doing ' . . . he will set him over all that he hath. But if that evil servant shall begin to beat his fellow servants . . . the lord of that servant shall cut him asunder.
Luke xii.	42 }	

' And that servant, which knew his lord's will, and made not ready, nor did according to his will, shall be beaten with many stripes. But he that knew not, and did things worthy of stripes, shall be beaten with few stripes. And to whomsoever much is given, of him shall much be required ; and to whom they commit much, of him will they ask the more.'

Luke xii.   37   ' Blessed are those servants, whom the lord . . . shall find watching.'

Matt.xxv.14-30   ' For the kingdom of heaven is as a man travelling into a far country, who called his own servants, and delivered unto them his goods.

' And unto one he gave five talents, to another two, and to another one ; to every man according to his several ability ; and straightway took his journey.

' Then he that had received the five talents went and traded with the same, and made them other five talents.

' And likewise he that had received two, he also gained other two.

' But he that had received one went and digged in the earth, and hid his lord's money.

' After a long time the lord of those servants cometh, and reckoneth with them.

' And so he that had received five talents came and brought other five talents, saying, Lord, thou deliveredst unto me five talents ; behold, I have gained beside them five talents more.

' His lord said unto him, Well done, thou good and faithful servant : thou hast been faithful over a few things, I will make thee ruler over many things : enter thou into the joy of thy lord.

' He also that had received two talents came and said, Lord, thou deliveredst unto me two talents :

Matt.xxv.14-30
(continued)

behold, I have gained two other talents beside them.

' His lord said unto him, Well done, good and faithful servant ; thou hast been faithful over a few things, I will make thee ruler over many things : enter thou into the joy of thy lord.

' Then he which had received the one talent came and said, Lord, I knew thee that thou art an hard man, reaping where thou hast not sown, and gathering where thou hast not strawed :

' And I was afraid, and went and hid thy talent in the earth : lo, there thou hast that is thine.

' His lord answered and said unto him, Thou wicked and slothful servant, thou knewest that I reap where I sowed not, and gather where I have not strawed :

' Thou oughtest therefore to have put my money to the exchangers [bankers, R.V.], and then at my coming I should have received mine own with usury [interest, R.V.].

' Take therefore the talent from him, and give it unto him which hath ten talents.

' For unto every one that hath shall be given, and he shall have abundance : but from him that hath not shall be taken away even that which he hath.

' And cast ye the unprofitable servant into outer darkness : there shall be weeping and gnashing of teeth.'

Luke xix. 12-27

' A certain nobleman went into a far country to receive for himself a kingdom, and to return.

' And he called his ten servants and delivered them ten pounds, and said unto them, Occupy till I come.

' But his citizens hated him, and sent a message after him, saying, We will not have this man to reign over us.

' And it came to pass, that when he was returned, having received the kingdom, then he commanded these servants to be called unto him, to whom he had given the money, that he might know how much every man had gained by trading.

' Then came the first, saying, Lord, thy pound hath gained ten pounds.

' And he said unto him, Well, thou good servant : because thou hast been faithful in a very little, have thou authority over ten cities.

' And the second came, saying, Lord, thy pound hath gained five pounds.

' And he said likewise to him, Be thou also over five cities.

' And another came, saying, Lord, behold, here is thy pound, which I have kept laid up in a napkin :

' For I feared thee, because thou art an austere man : thou takest up that thou layedst not down, and reapest that thou didst not sow.

' And he saith unto him, Out of thine own mouth will I judge thee, thou wicked servant. Thou knewest that

Luke xix. 12-27
(*continued*)

I was an austere man, taking up that I laid not down, and reaping that I did not sow :

' Wherefore then gavest not thou my money into the bank, that at my coming I might have required mine own with usury ?

' And he said unto them that stood by, Take from him the pound, and give it to him that hath ten pounds.

' (And they said unto him, Lord, he hath ten pounds.)

' For I say unto you, That unto every one which hath shall be given ; and from him that hath not, even that he hath shall be taken away from him.

' But those mine enemies, which would not that I should reign over them, bring hither, and slay them before me.'

OTHER REFERENCES TO SERVANTS AND STEWARDS

Mark i. 20

James and John ' left their father Zebedee in the boats with the hired servants . . .'

Mark xii. 2

The vineyard owner sent his servant to collect his revenues from the husbandmen—then a second and third and many others ; all were killed. Finally his son.

Matt. xiii. 27

The servants of the householder came and said unto him, ' Sir, didst thou not sow good seed in thy field ? ' &c.

Matt. xviii.

Parable of the Unmerciful Servant (*vide* CONTRACT AND SERVICE).

Matt. xxii. 8 ⎫ Luke xiv. ⎭	*Parable of the Marriage Feast.* Servants went out into the highways, and gathered together the guests.
Luke xvi. 1-13	' And he said also unto his disciples, ' There was a certain rich man, which had a steward ; and the same was accused unto him that he had wasted his goods.

' And he called him, and said unto him, How is it that I hear this of thee? give an account of thy stewardship ; for thou mayest be no longer steward. Then the steward said within himself, What shall I do ? for my lord taketh away from me the stewardship : I cannot dig ; to beg I am ashamed. I am resolved what to do, that, when I am put out of the stewardship, they may receive me into their houses.

' So he called every one of his lord's debtors unto him, and said unto the first, How much owest thou unto my lord ?

' And he said, An hundred measures of oil. And he said unto him, Take thy bill, and sit down quickly, and write fifty.

' Then said he to another, And how much owest thou ? And he said, An hundred measures of wheat. And he said unto him, Take thy bill, and write fourscore.

' And the lord commended the unjust steward, because he had done wisely ; for the children of this

Luke xvi. 1-13
(*continued*)

world are in their generation wiser than the children of light.

' And I say unto you, Make to yourselves friends of the mammon of unrighteousness ; that, when ye fail, they may receive you into everlasting habitations.

' He that is faithful in that which is least is faithful also in much : and he that is unjust in the least is unjust also in much.

' If therefore ye have not been faithful in the unrighteous mammon, who will commit to your trust the true riches ?

' And if ye have not been faithful in that which is another man's, who shall give you that which is your own ?

' No servant can serve two masters : for either he will hate the one, and love the other ; or else he will hold to the one, and despise the other. Ye cannot serve God and mammon.'

Luke xvii. 7-10

' But which of you, having a servant plowing or feeding cattle, will say unto him by and by, when he is come from the field, Go and sit down to meat;

' And will not rather say unto him, Make ready wherewith I may sup, and gird thyself, and serve me, till I have eaten and drunken ; and afterward thou shalt eat and drink ?

' Doth he thank that servant because he did the things that were commanded him ?   I trow not.

Luke xvii. 7-10 *(continued)*		' So likewise ye, when ye shall have done all those things which are commanded you, say, We are unprofitable servants : we have done that which was our duty to do.'
John xiii. xv.	16 } 20	' The servant is not greater than his lord.'
	15	' Henceforth I call you not servants.'
John x.	11	' The good shepherd giveth his life for the sheep.'
	13	' The hireling fleeth, because he is an hireling, and careth not for the sheep.'

LENDING AND DEBTORS

Luke vii.	41	One who was forgiven five hundred pence and the other fifty—the former ' will love him most.'
Luke xii. Matt. v.	59 } 26	' Agree with thine adversary . . . lest thou be cast into prison . . . thou shalt by no means come out thence till thou hast paid the [very] [last mite] [farthing].'
Matt. v.	42	' And from him that would borrow from thee, turn thou not away.'
Luke vi.	34	' And if ye lend to them of whom ye hope to receive, what thank have ye ? even sinners lend to sinners, to receive again as much.'

BUYING AND SELLING

Matt. x. Luke xii.	29 } 6	' Are not two sparrows sold for a farthing ? '
		' Are not five sparrows sold for two farthings ? '

Mark xi.	15 ⎫	' And he entered into the temple, and
Matt. xxi.	12 ⎬	began to cast out them that sold and
Luke xix.	45 ⎭	bought in the temple, and overthrew the tables of the money-changers and the seats of them that sold doves.'

John ii.	16	' Make not my Father's house a house of merchandise.'

Mark vi.	37 ⎫	*The Feeding of the Five Thousand.*
Matt. xiv.	16 ⎪	' Shall we go and buy two hundred
Luke ix.	13 ⎬	pennyworth of bread, and give them
John vi.	⎭	to eat ? '

Mark viii.	8 ⎫	*The Feeding of the Four Thousand.*
Matt. xv.	37 ⎭	

Luke x.	35	' And on the morrow he took out two pence and gave them to the host, and said, Take care of him ; and whatsoever thou spendest more, I, when I come back again, will repay thee.'

EMPLOYMENT OF MONEY (*Interest*)

Matt. xxv.	27 ⎫	*Parable of the Talents.* ' Thou
Luke xix.	23 ⎭	oughtest therefore to have put my money to the bankers, and at my coming I should have received back my own with interest.'

BENEVOLENCE AND THE SPIRIT OF GIVING

Matt. v.	42 ⎫	' Give to him that asketh thee, and
Luke vi.	30 ⎭	from him that would borrow of thee turn thou not away . . . [and of him that taketh away thy goods, ask them not again].'

P M

Matt. vi.   3-4   'When thou doest alms, let not thy left hand know what thy right hand doeth : that thine alms may be in secret.'

Luke xiv.   12   'When thou makest a dinner or a supper, call not thy friends, nor thy brethren, nor thy kinsmen, nor rich neighbours ; lest haply they also bid thee again, and a recompense be made thee.   But when thou makest a feast, bid the poor, the maimed, the lame, the blind : And thou shalt be blessed, because they have not wherewith to recompense thee.'

ECONOMIC PREVISION

Luke xiv. 28-33   'For which of you, intending to build a tower, sitteth not down first, and counteth the cost, whether he have sufficient to finish it ?

'Lest haply, after he hath laid the foundation, and is not able to finish it, all that behold it begin to mock him,

'Saying, This man began to build, and was not able to finish.

'Or what king, going to make war against another king, sitteth not down first, and consulteth whether he be able with ten thousand to meet him that cometh against him with twenty thousand ?

'Or else, while the other is yet a great way off, he sendeth an embassage, and desireth conditions of peace.

'So likewise, whosoever he be of you that forsaketh not all that he hath, he cannot be my disciple.'

TAXES, CIVIC AUTHORITY, &C.

Matt. xxiii. 23 ⎱ Luke xi. 42 ⎰	'For ye tithe mint [and anise and cummin] [and rue and every herb], and have left undone the weightier matters of the law . . . but these ought ye to have done, and not to leave the other undone.'
Luke xi. 46	'Woe unto you lawyers also, for ye lade men with burdens grievous to be borne, and ye yourselves touch not the burdens with one of your fingers.'
Luke iii. 14	To the publicans : ' Extort no more than that which is appointed you.' To the soldiers : ' Neither exact anything wrongfully, and be content with your wages.'
Mark xii. 14-17 ⎫ Matt.xxii.17-21 ⎬ Luke xx. 22-5 ⎭	' Is it lawful to give tribute [κῆνσον, Matt. and Mark, φόρον, Luke] unto Caesar or not ? ' . . . ' Whose image and superscription hath it ? . . . Then render unto Caesar the things that are Caesar's, and unto God the things that are God's.'

MATERIAL NECESSITIES AND RELIGIOUS FORMALITY

Mark ii. 25-6 ⎫ Matt. xii. 3-4 ⎬ Luke vi. 3-4 ⎭	The incident of satisfying hunger (a) on the Sabbath, (b) by taking the shewbread. ' The sabbath was made for man, and not man for the sabbath.'
Mark iii. 4 ⎫ Matt. xii. 11 ⎪ Luke vi. 9 ⎬ xiii. 15 ⎪ xiv. 5 ⎭	It is lawful on the Sabbath to do good and to save life, to loose the ox or ass from the stall and lead him away to watering, or to rescue either if ' fallen into a well.'

| Mark vii. | 11 ⎤ |
| Matt. xv. | 5 ⎦ |

'But ye say, If a man shall say to his father or his mother, That wherewith thou mightest have been profited by me is Corban, that is to say, Given to God; ye no longer suffer him to do aught for his father or his mother; making void the word of God by your tradition.'

NEIGHBOURS

Mark xii.	31 ⎤
Matt. xxii.	38 ⎬
Luke x.	27 ⎦

The Second Commandment. 'Thou shalt love thy neighbour as thyself' ... 'much more than all whole burnt offerings and sacrifices' ... 'on these two commandments hangeth the whole law and the prophets.'

Luke x. 30-5

'A certain man went down from Jerusalem to Jericho, and fell among thieves, which stripped him of his raiment, and wounded him, and departed, leaving him half dead.

'And by chance there came down a certain priest that way: and when he saw him, he passed by on the other side.

'And likewise a Levite, when he was at the place, came and looked on him, and passed by on the other side.

'But a certain Samaritan, as he journeyed, came where he was: and when he saw him, he had compassion on him,

'And went to him, and bound up his wounds, pouring in oil and wine, and set him on his own beast and brought him to an inn, and took care of him.

Luke x.   30-5   ' And on the morrow when he de-
(continued)   parted, he took out two pence, and
gave them to the host, and said unto
him, Take care of him ; and whatsoever thou spendest more, when I
come again, I will repay thee.'

CAUSE AND EFFECT

Matt. iii.   10 ⎫ ' Every tree therefore that bringeth
Luke iii.   9 ⎭ not forth good fruit is hewn down,
and cast into the fire.'

Mark iv.   24 ⎫ ' With what measure ye mete, it
Matt. vii.   2*b* ⎬ shall be measured unto you . . . and
Luke vi.   38*b* ⎭ more shall be given unto you . . . it
shall be measured to you again . . .
and all these things shall be added
unto you.'

Matt. vii.   16 ⎫ ' The tree is known by its fruit. . . .'
       xii.   33 ⎬ ' Therefore by their fruits ye shall
Luke vi.   44 ⎭ know them.'

Luke vi.   45*b*   ' The good man out of [the good
treasure of his heart] [his good treas-
ure] bringeth forth that which is
good.'

Matt. xii.   33   ' The tree is known by its fruit.'

Luke vi.   38 ⎫ ' For with what measure ye mete, it
Matt. vii.   2 ⎭ shall be measured to you again.'

Luke xiii.   9   *Parable of the Fig Tree.* ' Lord, let it
alone this year also, till I shall dig
about it, and dung it : and if it bear
fruit thenceforth, well ; but if not,
thou shalt cut it down.'

| John xv. | 2 | ' Every branch in me that beareth not fruit he taketh away; and every branch that beareth fruit, he purgeth it, that it may bring forth more fruit.' |

LIMITATIONS OF MATERIAL THINGS

| Matt. iv. | 4 ⎫ | ' Man shall not live by bread |
| Luke iv. | 4 ⎭ | alone. . . . ' |

| Matt. iv. | 8 ⎫ | ' The devil . . . sheweth him all the |
| Luke iv. | 5 ⎭ | kingdoms of the world and the glory of them.' |

| Matt. xxiv. | 38 ⎫ | *An Eschatological Discourse.* ' Like- |
| Luke xvii. | 28 ⎭ | wise even as it came to pass in the days of Lot : they ate, they drank, they bought, they sold, they planted, they builded, but in the day Lot went out from Sodom, it rained fire and brimstone and destroyed them all.' |

| John vi. | 27 | ' Labour not for the meat which perisheth.' |

| John iv. | 38 | ' I sent you to reap that whereon ye bestowed no labour; other men laboured, and ye are entered into their labours.' |

THE PRODIGAL SON

| Luke xv. 11-19 | ' And he said, A certain man had two sons : |
| | ' And the younger of them said to his father, Father, give me the portion of goods that falleth to me. And he divided unto them his living. |

Luke xv. 11-19
(continued)

'And not many days after the younger son gathered all together, and took his journey into a far country, and there wasted his substance with riotous living.

'And when he had spent all, there arose a mighty famine in that land ; and he began to be in want.

'And he went and joined himself to a citizen of that country ; and he sent him into his fields to feed swine.

'And he would fain have filled his belly with the husks that the swine did eat : and no man gave unto him.

'And when he came to himself, he said, How many hired servants of my father's have bread enough and to spare, and I perish with hunger !

'I will arise and go to my father, and will say unto him, Father, I have sinned against heaven, and before thee,

'And am no more worthy to be called thy son : make me as one of thy hired servants. . . .

22-31

'But the father said to his servants, Bring forth the best robe, and put it on him ; and put a ring on his hand, and shoes on his feet :

'And bring hither the fatted calf, and kill it ; and let us eat, and be merry :

'For this my son was dead, and is alive again ; he was lost, and is found. And they began to be merry.

'Now his elder son was in the field : and as he came and drew nigh to the

Luke xv. 22-31
(*continued*)

house, he heard musick and dancing.

' And he called one of the servants, and asked what these things meant.

' And he said unto him, Thy brother is come ; and thy father hath killed the fatted calf, because he had received him safe and sound.

' And he was angry, and would not go in : therefore came his father out, and intreated him.

' And he answering said to his father, Lo, these many years do I serve thee, neither transgressed I at any time thy commandment : and yet thou never gavest me a kid, that I might make merry with my friends :

' But as soon as this thy son was come, which hath devoured thy living with harlots, thou hast killed for him the fatted calf.

' And he said unto him, Son, thou art ever with me, and all that I have is thine.'

MARRIAGE AT CANA

John ii.   1-10

' And the third day there was a marriage in Cana of Galilee ; and the mother of Jesus was there :

' And both Jesus was called, and his disciples, to the marriage.

' And when they wanted wine, the mother of Jesus saith unto him, They have no wine.

' Jesus saith unto her, Woman, what have I to do with thee ? mine hour is not yet come.

John ii.   1-10
(*continued*)

' His mother saith unto the servants, Whatsoever he saith unto you, do it.

' And there were set there six water-pots of stone, after the manner of the purifying of the Jews, containing two or three firkins apiece.

' Jesus saith unto them, Fill the waterpots with water. And they filled them up to the brim.

' And he saith unto them, Draw out now, and bear unto the governor of the feast. And they bare it.

' When the ruler of the feast had tasted the water that was made wine, and knew not whence it was : (but the servants which drew the water knew ;) the governor of the feast called the bridegroom,

' And saith unto him, Every man at the beginning doth set forth good wine ; and when men have well drunk, then that which is worse : but thou hast kept the good wine until now.'

GENERAL

Luke vi.   31

' And as ye would that men should do to you, do ye also to them like-wise.'

Mark ix.   41 ⎱
Matt. x.   42 ⎰

' For whosoever shall give you a cup of water to drink . . . because ye are Christ's, I say unto you shall in no wise lose his reward.'

Mark vii.   27 ⎱
Matt. xv.   26 ⎰

' Let the children first be filled : for it is not meet to take the children's bread and cast it to the dogs.'

Mark xii.	40 ⎫	'Beware of the scribes, which . . .
Matt. xxiii.	14 ⎬	devour widows' houses . . . these shall
Luke xx.	47 ⎭	receive greater condemnation.'

Matt. v.   7   'Blessed are the merciful, for they shall obtain mercy.'

xxv.   42   'For I was an hungered, and ye gave me no meat,' &c.

Mark viii.	17 ⎫	'Beware of the leaven of the Phari-
Matt. xvi.	8 ⎬	sees. . . .'

'And they reasoned one with another saying, We have no bread.'

Mark vi.	11 ⎫	'Take nothing for your journey,
Matt. x.	14 ⎬	neither staff, nor bread, nor wallet,
Luke ix.	4 ⎬	nor money, neither have two coats.
x.	5 ⎭	[Salute no man by the way.]

'And as many as receive you not, when ye depart from that city, shake off the dust from your feet for a testimony against them.'

John xxi.   *The Great Draught of Fishes.*

II. THE NEW TESTAMENT (AFTER THE GOSPELS)

THE RICH

1 Tim. vi.   8   'Having food and raiment let us be therewith content.

9   'But they that will be rich fall into temptation and a snare. . . .

10   'For the love of money is the root of all evil.'

1 Tim. vi.	17	' Charge them that are rich in this world, that they be not highminded, nor trust in uncertain riches, but in the living God, who giveth us richly all things to enjoy ;
	18	' That they do good, that they be rich in good works, ready to distribute, willing to communicate. . . .'
Jas. i.	9	' Let the brother of low degree rejoice in that he is exalted :
	10	' But the rich, in that he is made low : because as the flower of the grass he shall pass away.
	11	' For the sun is no sooner risen with a burning heat, but it withereth the grass . . . so also shall the rich man fade away in his ways.'
ii.	2	' If there come into your assembly a man with a gold ring, in goodly apparel, and there come in also a poor man in vile raiment ;
	3	' And ye have respect to him that weareth the gay clothing, and say unto him, Sit here in a good place ; and say to the poor, Stand thou there, or sit here under my footstool :
	4	' Are ye not then partial in yourselves . . . ? '
	6	' But ye have despised the poor. Do not rich men oppress you, and draw you before the judgment seats ? '
	9	' But if ye have respect to persons, ye commit sin. . . .'

Jas. v.   1   ' Go to now, ye rich men, weep and howl for your miseries that shall come upon you.

              2   ' Your riches are corrupted, and your garments are motheaten.

              3   ' Your gold and silver is cankered ; and the rust of them shall be a witness against you, and shall eat your flesh as it were fire. Ye have heaped treasure together for the last days.

              4   ' Behold, the hire of the labourers who have reaped down your fields, which is of you kept back by fraud, crieth.'

RICHES AND POVERTY CONTRASTED

2 Cor. viii.   9   ' Though he was rich, yet for your sakes he became poor, that ye through his poverty might be rich.'

THE POOR AND POVERTY

Gal. ii.   10   ' Only they would that we should remember the poor ; the same which I also was forward to do.'

SERVANTS AND SERVICE AND MASTERS

Rom. xiv.   4   ' Who art thou that judgest another man's servant ? to his own master he standeth or falleth.'

1 Cor. iv.   2   ' Moreover it is required in stewards, that a man be found faithful.'

Gal. iv.   1   ' The heir, as long as he is a child, differeth nothing from a servant, though he be lord of all. . . .'

Gal. iv.	7	' Wherefore thou art no more a servant, but a son.'
Eph. vi.	5	' Servants, be obedient to them that are your masters according to the flesh, with fear and trembling, in singleness of your heart, as unto Christ.

[Also Col. iii. 22.]

	6	' Not with eyeservice, as men-pleasers ; but as the servants of Christ, doing the will of God from the heart ;
	7	' With good will doing service, as to the Lord, and not to men :
	8	' Knowing that whatsoever good thing any man doeth, the same shall he receive of the Lord, whether he be bond or free.
	9	' And, ye masters, do the same things unto them, forbearing threatening. . . .'
Col. iv.	1	' Masters, give unto your servants that which is just and equal.'
Titus ii.	9	' Exhort servants to be obedient unto their own masters, and to please them well in all things ; not answering again ;
	10	' Not purloining, but showing all good fidelity.'
iii.	1	' Put them in mind to be subject to principalities and powers, to obey magistrates. . . .'
1 Pet. ii.	18	'Servants, be subject to your masters with all fear ; not only to the good and gentle, but also to the froward

1 Pet. ii.	20	. . . if, when ye do well, and suffer for it, ye take it patiently, this is acceptable with God.'
Heb. xiii.	17	' Obey them that have the rule over you, and submit yourselves.'

COMMON OWNERSHIP

Acts ii.	44	' And all that believed were together, and had all things common ;
	45	' And sold their possessions and goods, and parted them to all men, as every man had need.'
iv.	34	' Neither was there any among them that lacked : for as many as were possessors of lands or houses sold them, and brought the prices of the things that were sold,
	35	' And laid them down at the apostles' feet : and distribution was made unto every man according as he had need.'
	37	Barnabas sold his land and brought the money to the apostles.
v.	2	Ananias ' kept back part of the price,' and lied about it.
viii.	20	' But Peter said, Thy money perish with thee, because thou hast thought that the gift of God may be purchased with money.'

CHARITY AND GIVING

Acts xx.	35	' It is more blessed to give than to receive.'
Rom. xii.	8	' He that giveth, let him do it with simplicity ; he that ruleth, with diligence.'

Rom. xii.	10	' Be kindly affectioned one to another with brotherly love ; in honour preferring one another.'
	13	' Distributing to the necessity of saints ; given to hospitality.'
	20	' If thine enemy hunger, feed him ; if he thirst, give him drink : for in so doing thou shalt heap coals of fire on his head.'
1 Cor. xiii.	3	' And though I bestow all my goods to feed the poor . . . and have not charity, it profiteth me nothing.'
2 Cor. ix.	7	' Every man according as he purposeth in his heart, so let him give ; not grudgingly, or of necessity : for God loveth a cheerful giver.
	8	' And God is able to make all grace abound toward you ; that ye, always having all sufficiency in all things, may abound to every good work :
	9	' As it is written, He hath dispersed abroad ; he hath given to the poor : his righteousness remaineth for ever . . .'
Eph. iv.	28	' Let him that stole steal no more : but rather let him labour, working with his hands the thing which is good, that he may have to give to him that needeth.'
Heb. xiii.	2	' Be not forgetful to entertain strangers. . . .
	3	' Remember them that are in bonds. . . .'

SUPPORT OF THE CHURCH

Rom. xv. 25 'But now I go unto Jerusalem to minister unto the saints.

26 'For it hath pleased them of Macedonia and Achaia to make a certain contribution for the poor saints which are at Jerusalem.

27 'It hath pleased them verily; and their debtors they are. For if the Gentiles have been made partakers of their spiritual things, their duty is also to minister unto them in carnal things.'

1 Cor. xvi. 1 'Now concerning the collection for the saints, as I have given order to the churches of Galatia, even so do ye.

2 'Upon the first day of the week let every one of you lay by him in store, as God hath prospered him, that there be no gatherings when I come.'

2 Cor. viii. 12 'For if there be first a willing mind, it is accepted according to that a man hath, and not according to that he hath not.

13 'For I mean not that other men be eased, and ye burdened:

14 'But by an equality, that now at this time your abundance may be a supply for their want, that their abundance also may be a supply for your want: that there may be equality:

15 'As it is written, He that had gathered much had nothing over; and he that had gathered little had no lack.'

2 Cor. viii.	20	' Avoiding this, that no man should blame us in this abundance which is administered by us :
	21	' Providing for honest things. . . .'
ix.	5	' Therefore I thought it necessary to exhort the brethren, that they would go before unto you, and make up beforehand your bounty, whereof ye had notice before, that the same might be ready, as a matter of bounty, and not as of covetousness.'
	12	' For the administration of this service not only supplieth the want of the saints, but is abundant also by many thanksgivings unto God ;
	13	' Whiles by the experiment of this ministration they glorify God . . . and for your liberal distribution unto them, and unto all men.'
xi.	8	' I robbed other churches, taking wages of them, to do you service.
	9	' And when I was present with you, and wanted, I was chargeable to no man : for that which was lacking to me the brethren which came from Macedonia supplied : and in all things I have kept myself from being burdensome unto you.'

[Also 2 Cor. xii. 13, 14.]

2 Thess. iii.	8	' Neither did we eat any man's bread for nought ; but wrought with labour and travail night and day, that we might not be chargeable to any of you:
	9	' Not because we have not power, but to make ourselves an ensample unto you to follow us.'

Q M

| Acts xx. | 33 | ' I have coveted no man's silver, or gold, or apparel. |
| | 34 | ' Yea, ye yourselves know, that these hands have ministered unto my necessities, and to them that were with me.' |

DIVISION OF FUNCTIONS

Rom. xii.	6	' Having then gifts differing according to the grace that is given to us, whether prophecy, let us prophesy, according to the proportion of faith ;
	7	' Or ministry, let us wait on our ministering : or he that teacheth, on teaching ;
	8	' Or he that exhorteth, on exhortation. . . .'

REFERENCE TO BUSINESS AND CRAFT

Rom. xii.	11	' Not slothful in business . . .'
Acts xviii.	3	The tentmakers—the same craft.
xix.	24	Demetrius—craftsman silversmith ; shrines for Diana.
	27	Craft in danger.

GIVING TRIBUTE AND DUES : AUTHORITIES

| Rom. xiii. | 7 | ' Render therefore to all their dues : tribute to whom tribute is due ; custom to whom custom ; fear to whom fear ; honour to whom honour. |
| | 8 | ' Owe no man anything, but to love one another.' |

1 Tim. ii.	1	'I exhort therefore, that, first of all, supplications, prayers, intercessions, and giving of thanks, be made for all men ;
	2	'For kings, and for all that are in authority.'
1 Pet. ii.	13	'Submit yourselves to every ordinance of man for the Lord's sake : whether it be to the king, as supreme ;
	14	'Or unto governors . . . and for the praise of them that do well.'

LABOUR AND EQUIVALENT REWARD

1 Cor. iii.	7	'So then neither is he that planteth any thing, neither he that watereth ; but God that giveth the increase.
	8	'Now he that planteth and he that watereth are one : and every man shall receive his own reward according to his own labour.'
2 Cor. ix.	6	'But this I say, He which soweth sparingly shall reap also sparingly ; and he which soweth bountifully shall reap also bountifully.'
2 Thess. iii.	10	'For even when we were with you, this we commanded you, that if any would not work, neither should he eat.
	11	'For we hear that there are some which walk among you disorderly, working not at all, but are busybodies.
	12	'Now them that are such we command and exhort by our Lord Jesus Christ, that with quietness they work, and eat their own bread.'

Qᴍ*

1 Tim. v.	18	' For the scripture saith, Thou shalt not muzzle the ox that treadeth out the corn. And, The labourer is worthy of his reward.'
2 Tim. ii.	6	' The husbandman that laboureth must be first partaker of the fruits.'
1 Cor. ix.	6	' Or I only and Barnabas, have not we power to forbear working ?
	7	' Who goeth a warfare any time at his own charges ? who planteth a vineyard, and eateth not the fruit thereof ? or who feedeth a flock, and eateth not of the milk of the flock ? '
	9	' For it is written in the law of Moses, Thou shalt not muzzle the mouth of the ox that treadeth out the corn.'

GOING TO LAW

1 Cor. vi.	1	' Dare any of you, having a matter against another, go to law before the unjust, and not before the saints ? '
	7	' Now therefore there is utterly a fault among you, because ye go to law one with another. Why do ye not rather take wrong ? why do ye not rather suffer yourselves to be defrauded ? '

GENERAL

Acts xxvii.	38	Casting the wheat into the sea to lighten the ship.
Rom. xii.	17	' Recompense to no man evil for evil. Provide things honest in the sight of all men.'

Rom. xiv. 21   ' It is good neither to eat flesh, nor to drink wine, nor any thing whereby thy brother stumbleth, or is offended, or is made weak.'

xv. 1   ' We then that are strong ought to bear the infirmities of the weak, and not to please ourselves.'

1 Cor. x. 24   ' Let no man seek his own, but every man another's *wealth.*' [R.V., 'good'; Moffatt, 'interests.']

33   ' Even as I please all men in all things, not seeking mine own profit, but the profit of many, that they may be saved.'

Titus i. 10-11   ' For there are many unruly and vain talkers and deceivers . . . teaching things which they ought not, for filthy lucre's sake.'

1 Pet. v. 2   ' Feed the flock of God which is among you, taking the oversight thereof, not by constraint, but willingly ; not for filthy lucre, but of a ready mind.'

APPENDIX II

SOCIAL CREDIT

THE Social Credit Scheme is the name given to the diagnosis of our economic ills, and the particular remedies suggested for them, which, while now sprouting out into various proposals, owe their origin to Major C. H. Douglas. His training was a considerable experience in practical engineering with the Westinghouse companies in America and India, as a railway engineer, and then as Assistant Superintendent of the R.A. Factory, Farnborough, during the war. It was while engaged upon this work, and especially the accountancy side, that he came to observe that the total costs incurred in any period rather obviously included more than wages and salaries—there were payments for rent and rates, raw materials, dividends, &c. Prices of goods produced had to cover costs, if the business was to go on, but all that was available to buy the finished goods was the wages and salaries and dividends. If this were true for every productive business, then, *adding them all together*, the whole idea upon which our system is supposed to work, viz. that all costs are distributed as purchasing power, would fall to the ground. When he collected information from a hundred large businesses, he found in every case that the total costs were greater than the sums paid out for wages, salaries, and dividends. In cases where losses were being made, costs were in excess of prices, but generally the wages, salaries, and dividends were inadequate to buy the products. He published his conclusion, in the *English Review*, that we are living under a system of accountancy which renders the delivery of the nation's goods and services to itself a technical impossibility. For a time the progress of the idea was slow, but his admirers hailed him as the ' Einstein of Economics.' In various books and pamphlets he and his supporters elaborated the idea, and the remedy. The cure was to ' create ' purchasing power enough to make good the deficiency, and this has blossomed forth into National Dividends, and other schemes for preventing 'poverty in the midst of plenty.'

After a time, especially with the world depression, when men are naturally eager to seize any remedy which looks plausible—and how plausible this really looked !—the ideas spread rapidly and captured the imagination of parts of Canada, New Zealand, and, to a less extent, Australia. In England, by 1931, the movement was sufficiently formidable and important for the Macmillan Commission on Finance—composed of men of all views—to give a serious hearing to its exponents, and no one studying the subject should fail to read the evidence and cross-examination. It can be found conveniently analysed in a book, *Social Credits or Socialism*, by W. R. Hiskett, a member of the Socialist Party and a critic of the existing banking régime. The proposals received no kind of support or sympathy from the Commission, after a most patient examination. Dr. Hugh Dalton, in a preface to this work, says of the evidence given by Major Douglas : ' The impression which this performance creates upon my mind is that of an incurably muddleheaded witness, who has never really thought out either the theoretical or the practical implications of his proposals, but flounders under cross-examination from one confused evasion to another. I fancy that most readers of this book, even if they start with some degree of sympathy for Major Douglas's ideas, will end by forming a similar impression to my own.'

The Labour Party had already in 1922 issued a report

analysing the scheme carefully and reporting that it was 'theoretically unsound and unworkable in practice,' and that it was ' out of harmony with the trend of labour thought, and indeed fundamentally opposed to the principles for which the Labour Party stands.'

Dr. Dalton had no hesitation in reporting thirteen years later that ' the Douglas scheme is not only an intellectual nightmare, but an administrative monstrosity . . . the proposals start from a false diagnosis of our economic illness and end with an absurd plan of treatment, which cannot, in practice, be applied and, if it could, would make the patient much worse.'

Powerful advocacy has come from the Dean of Canterbury, also a trained engineer. The movement has spread and in Alberta has captured the electorate. In New Zealand it causes much unrest in thought, and it counts its adherents in the United States—under Townsend and other allied schemes—by the million. Certain parts of the diagnosis of the nature of the machine seemed to coincide with that made by others dealing with causes of the depression, so that it became confused and held a place amongst ' underconsumption ' theories of various kinds. The professional academic world held aloof, just discussing it in a few words in their lectures, as ' unsound,' until the last three years, during which a number of them, especially the younger ones from different schools of thought, have given a thorough analysis with a complete unanimity of conclusion.[1] The diagnosis and the remedy are alike condemned by the whole academic world. Major Douglas has, therefore, most of the qualifications of a martyr, and his supporters continue vigorously to urge his claims.

[1] *Vide* especially Hiskett, *Social Credits or Socialism*, 1935 ; Maurice Dobb, *Social Credit Discredited*, 1936 ; E. F. Nash, *Machines and Purchasing Power*, 1935 ; John Strachey in a pamphlet, *Social Credit*, 1936 ; Professor Copland, *Facts and Fallacies of Social Credit* (Melbourne) ; H. M. Gaitskell on ' Four Economic Heretics,' in *All about Money*, ed. G. D. H. Cole.

It is not my intention to duplicate by a detailed analysis the excellent works referred to, but only to indicate briefly the *nature of the problems involved*, in order that the distinction between method and motive made in this book can be more easily illustrated. It will be seen that Major Douglas's theory applies both outside and inside times of depression, with good men and with bad. He does not base anything upon the evil of maldistribution or competition, or prevailing motives of private profit. The nearest he gets to anything curable along the line of motive is where his advocates abuse the existing banking system in terms which really accuse its supporters of so much unnecessary obscurantism and dullness of wits as to amount to moral obliquity, clinging to ' money power,' and the obtuseness of a complacent vested interest. For example : ' For instance, it is simply childish to say that a country has no money for social betterment, or for any other purpose, when it has the skill, the men, and the material and plant to create that betterment. The banks or the Treasury can create the money in five minutes, and are doing it every day, and have been doing it for centuries ' (*The Douglas Manual*, which gives selections from his various books, p. 13). ' The banker, being essentially a dealer in a commodity called money, is fundamentally concerned to make that commodity as valuable as possible.' ' Why, then, is there so great a misdirection of attention in a matter of such primary importance ? There is, I think, only one general and comprehensive answer which can be given to this question : and that is that, whether consciously or not, there is a widespread feeling on the part of executives of all descriptions that the only method by which large masses of human beings can be kept in agreement with dogmatic moral and social ideals is by arranging that they shall be kept so hard at work that they have not the leisure or even the desire to think for themselves.'

' For instance, Mr. Snowden, the Socialist Chancellor of the Exchequer, in the *Banker* for May 1927, remarks of the Bank of England (an institution perhaps responsible for more economic misery than any which has ever existed) that it is " perhaps the greatest moral authority in the world." '

' . . . a halt will be called to the aggression of the financier, sanctioned and assisted by the law, upon each section of society in turn, and he will be reminded of the warning given many hundreds of years ago : " Ye take too much upon yourselves, ye sons of Levi." '

' While grave criticism of the personnel of the banking system, and its prostitution to politics, of a peculiarly vicious character is becoming daily more common and seems in many cases to be justified, it is evident that the world is becoming daily less willing to trust *any* personnel with a system at once so powerful, irresponsible, and convulsive in its operation.'

' The multiplication of the category of criminal offences, from cocaine-running to " long-firm " frauds, can be directly and solely traced to a deficiency of purchasing power and the vital necessity to expand it, honestly if possible, but to expand it anyway.'

All this is mild enough. Indeed, several times Major Douglas has gone out of his way to state explicitly that he is not accusing bankers and professors of moral perversity, but only of being slaves to the machine and, of course, intellectually muddled. The engineers treat the question as one of machinery. But the ministers of religion import a good deal more moral blame into the picture. The Dean says : ' Now those who manufacture money and throw it on the market, or withdraw it from the market at their discretion, exercise sovereign powers : they control prices ; they regulate wages ; they create, if they choose, wholesale unemployment ; and, at a price, and in favourable circumstances, employment too. When banks secured the power of money creation—one of the primary functions of a sovereign State—they secured power also to cause inflation or deflation, to send prices soaring or bring them tumbling down, the power to fling a country into unemployment and lead industry and agriculture to the verge of ruin. . . . Bank directors associate themselves actively in commercial enterprises. They are in the position, therefore—*should they choose to exercise it*—to create money for their own, or withhold it from their rivals', enterprises.'

The Rev. John Knowles puts the Bank and the Church in opposition : ' Those who value the Church should awake in time. It will be too late to save her when her foundations have been undermined by her rival. The really important point is that the morality of persuasion, which the Church at her best always stood for, is to be replaced by the morality of coercion ; for, whatever may be the moral authority of the Bank, no one will imagine that it is exercised by persuasion. . . . We do not suggest that the gentlemen who direct the Bank of England are the only people who belie our faith in the decency of human nature. We have no doubt they are amiable men who wish well to their fellows, relieve the poor according to their ability, and grieve at the moral chaos and material misery that abound. They, too, are in the grip of the system. In its grip because they believe in it, and because they have a vested interest in believing in it. Vested interests blind the eyes. . . . We have tried to show, though briefly, how the Financial System controls the screw, and keeps up a steady and ever increasing pressure on men to commit sin. . . .

' Finance will have none of your " change of heart." True, talking about it is allowable. Indeed, it is quite a useful diversion. . . . Therefore, there is no room in the system for real " life changers," or " changed lives." . . . So, we feel sure, the Directors of the Bank of England do not realize that while the Gadarene System besought Christ to depart, the Banking System compels

Christ to go, not only from " dark Satanic mills," but also from " England's pleasant pastures." '

Father Drinkwater is also unable to condone the existing financial system as bad mechanics without bringing in bad morals : ' For several centuries, in all lands, the civil law has made things easy for the usurer, and the intricacies of modern finance ; has laid down a rough-and-ready rule that there is no need for confessors to disturb the conscience of Catholics who are getting interest on their money in ways legalized by the civil law. But this does not mean that interest-taking is the only way in which the Money Power may commit injustice. Nor does it mean that there is no need for people to trouble about the justice or injustice of the laws of their country. On the contrary, if the Church is prepared to tolerate in practice what the civil law permits, there is all the more need for Catholics to study the effect of the existing laws from the point of view of social and distributive justice, and, if necessary, to work with others to " change the system." '

.   .   .   .

Major Douglas's case rests in the main on his famous theorem which can best be stated in his own words :

Rates of Flow of Prices and Purchasing Power. A factory or other productive organization has, besides its economic function as a producer of goods, a financial aspect—it may be regarded, on the one hand, as a device for the distribution of purchasing power to individuals through the media of wages, salaries, and dividends ; and on the other hand as a manufactory of prices—financial values. From this standpoint its payments may be divided into two groups :
Group A—All payments made to individuals (wages, salaries, and dividends).
Group B—All payments made to other organizations (raw materials, bank charges, and other external costs).
Now *the rate of flow of purchasing power to individuals is represented by A, but, since all payments go into prices, the*

rate of flow of prices cannot be less than A + B. The product of any factory may be considered as something which the public ought to be able to buy, although in many cases it is an intermediate product of no use to individuals, but only to a subsequent manufacture ; but, since A will not purchase A + B, a proportion of the product at least equivalent to B must be distributed by a form of purchasing power which is not comprised in the descriptions grouped under A. It will be necessary at a later stage to show that this additional purchasing power is provided by loan credit (bank overdrafts) or export credit.

The fallacy in this theorem has often been exposed, yet thousands have still never realized it. There is so much obscurity of expression that the idea is elusive, and many think that it is some deep truth that is enunciated. For Major Douglas himself says that his theory 'is one of those conceptions which, like the differential co-efficient in mathematics, to which it has a strong family resemblance, comes suddenly rather than by intellectual explanation.' The fallacy is that it ignores the point that in the final analysis all B payments become A payments. 'What appears as a B payment at a *later* stage of production represents an equivalent A payment at an earlier stage of production ' (Dobb). It is the fallacy of composition referred to so often in this book—what is true of each part taken separately is not true of all the parts combined in one whole. For the firms in industry taken all together, 'all payments ultimately become A payments and B payments do not exist.' If we have a string of firms at different stages of industry supplying from one to the other, the A payments seem to come out at the end, and there are *lots* of intermediate B payments, each set of A payments being insufficient to cover costs. But, if the firms were all in one combine, the B payments tend to disappear, and all come out as A payments. The theory thus overlooks the fact that if the concern X, producing for public consumption, is distributing goods for the purchase of which its A payments are insufficient, there are at the same moment a lot of firms (Y), not producing final goods for the public at all, which are distributing A payments, and *not* producing goods for these *A* payments to buy (B payments are meeting them). So these surplus A payments from Y are available for the deficiency of purchasing power in the business X.

Major Douglas replies (1) that, in any one period of time, A payments are less than total costs, for the A payments for earlier stages have been *used up*, and (2) that bank credits have to be raised to finance the stages of production, and this credit has to be repaid. This repayment, included in costs, does not get into purchasing power—it is dead. But these replies are even cruder fallacies than the old, and I must refer the reader to the works mentioned to get the information about the appropriate banking and industrial machinery which disposes of them.

Now, Major Douglas makes in substance five claims which have been conveniently summarized :

(1) That there is an inherent and continuous deficiency of purchasing power consequent on the non-availability, as purchasing power, of the whole of group B payments.
(2) That consumers' credits can be issued in such a form as not to produce inflation.
(3) That the rate of flow of purchasing power is much less than the rate of flow of prices.
(4) That production is almost entirely initiated by loan credit, and that this loan credit is issued by the banks, and to a very large extent repaid without producing payments to the public in the form of purchasing power.
(5) That the price level can be lowered by an issue of credit to the consumer.

Major Douglas holds that the deficiency of purchasing power must be made up by specially created consumer credit to bring it up to the total prices of commodities.

But he also holds that prices have to be artificially reduced *below* costs to bring them within purchasing power. So that we have a ' national dividend ' designed to give the consumer power to buy the goods that wages would leave unbought, but also industrial credit to reduce the goods in price to a point where the wages *can* buy them, and these alternative schemes intertwine in a baffling way. Mr. Nash ends : ' Thus our conclusion need not be subject to any doubt or qualification whatever. Social Credit is simply another name for continuous and progressive inflation. As the foundation for a reformed monetary system it is a fantastic absurdity.' Mr. Hiskett concludes : ' Unsound in theory and unworkable in practice.' Mr. Dobb, with strong Soviet sympathies, says that this ' sham enemy ' draws attention away from the real enemy. W. R. Lester, writing for the Henry George Foundation, says it is melancholy to think such fantastic arguments need refutation, when there are fundamental ends for which we should all be working ; and John Strachey is equally trenchant. From all points of view the verdict is the same : that the Douglas machine, as a machine, will not work because its construction is faulty, not because the motive power is inadequate or unsuitable. It is, therefore, idle to engage the sentiments, still less the passions, in recrimination. There are no more morals or ethics about it than there are about a locomotive. It *could* not be one of the better methods of a Christian order. It is no use condemning on moral grounds the methods that exist, simply because they might be improved if things that can never be, actually *could* be !

INDEX OF NAMES